OHIO

Cradle of Astronauts

How 26 Buckeyes Blazed the Trail for Life OFF Earth

Lisa Nicely

With Illustrations By William Hinsch

OHIO: Cradle of Astronauts, Copyright © 2024 by Learning Visuals

All rights reserved. Printed in the United States of America. No part of this book may be used or reproduced in any manner whatsoever without written permission except in the case of brief quotations embodied in critical articles or reviews.

For information contact: www.ohioastronauts.com

Book and Cover design by William D. Hinsch

ISBN: 979-8-35094-101-2

First Edition: January 2024

DEDICATION

For Carol, who's kept us all together and without whom this book would never have existed.

Table of Contents

A Stellar Legacy	7
John Glenn	11
Neil Armstrong	27
James Lovell	39
Judith Resnik	47
Eugene Kranz	55
Charles Bassett II	63
Sunita Williams	69
Terence 'Tom' Henricks	75
Dr. Karl Henize	83
Donn Eisele	91
Michael Gernhardt	99
Nancy Currie-Gregg	105
Robert Overmyer	113
Kenneth Cameron	119
G. David Low	127
Robert Springer	133
Mary Ellen Weber	141

Table of Contents

Ronald Sega	147
Ronald Parise	155
Gregory Harbaugh	161
Carl Walz	167
Donald Thomas	175
Gregory 'Box' Johnson	181
Michael 'Bueno' Good	187
Michael Foreman	195
Thomas Hennen	201
Honorary Buckeye Astronauts	205
Kathryn Sullivan	207
Kevin Kregel	213
Dr. Michael Barratt	219
Richard Linnehan	225
Douglas Wheelock	231
Astronomical possibilities	235
Acknowledgements	237
About The Author	240
About Bill Hinsch	241

"Don't give in to complacency and cynicism. Don't ignore what is bad, but concentrate on building what is good. Don't take America and the values reflected in our form of government for granted. And never forget that in our democracy, the government is not 'them. It is "us".

– John Glenn

A Stellar Legacy

Comedian Stephen Colbert once jokingly told U.S. Rep. Stephanie Tubbs-Jones of Ohio, "Twenty-two astronauts were born in Ohio. What is it about your state that makes people want to flee the Earth?"

Since NASA's inception, it has had more than 300 astronauts, twenty-five of whom came from Ohio with many more having Ohio ties. The question of why so many astronauts come from the Buckeye State has been asked by NASA, government officials, and others. In addition to astronauts, Ohio has provided NASA with invaluable support staff, including flight director Gene Kranz, planetary scientist Diana Blaney, chief engineer Marc Rayman, database manager Jill Noble, Space Science Project Office project manager James Withrow, Nancy Hall of the International Space Station and Human Health Office, and countless others.

So, what is it about Ohio that leads so many of its residents to become captivated by space exploration? It's a question with many possible answers, including a culture that values strong work ethic, having a unique outlook, willingness to take advantage of opportunities, even tradition.

Bill Barry, a NASA chief historian, has noted that the state has a "statistically significant" number of astronauts whose achievements are "a huge legacy for NASA." Ohioans have achieved many firsts for the organization – John Glenn, first American to orbit Earth; Neil Armstrong; first man to set foot on the moon; Michael Gernhardt, first U.S. space walk on the International Space Station; Terence Henricks, first person to log more than 1,000 hours as a Space Shuttle pilot/commander. Ohio has stood at the forefront of space and aviation since the beginning. Each Ohioan has built on a legacy that started with the Wright brothers, who invented and flew the first controlled airplane.

When NASA first held a press conference to introduce its Mercury 7 astronauts, Glenn said his motivation to join the program came from the brothers.

"I think we stand on the verge of something as big and as expansive as that was 50 years ago," he stated in 1959.

The Wright brothers are the reason why Ohio is called the "Birthplace of Aviation." In a forward to the book, Orbit of Discovery, Glenn stated, "Clearly Ohioans have a strong heritage of discovery and exploration is in their blood."

Ohioans are persistent in their dreams in the face of obstacles as well. Both Glenn and Armstrong have commented on jabs from other pilots about space travel being so easy "even a monkey can do it," referencing how nations sent monkeys into space prior to humans. The comments were probably colored with envy about not being chosen for the space program as well.

Ohioans have continued to add to the aeronautics tradition started by the Wright brothers.
Almost immediately after the brothers' successful flight, Ohioans were thinking of new ways to use flight. For example, just seven years after the Wright brothers' first flight, Ohio also boasted the first cargo flight when Philip Parmalee transported 10 bolts of fabric from Dayton to Columbus on Nov. 7, 1910, in a Wright Model B. It was the first of a growing aeronautic industry that continues today in the state.

Today, aeronautics is a big part of Ohio's economy. There are more than 60 companies that make up Ohio's space economy. In 2023, it was estimated that aerospace and defense made up 5.9 percent of the state's economy, while Ohio's colleges and universities produce more than 18,000 engineers and scientists a year. Those graduates help build aeronautics systems, vehicles, operational devices, and provide manpower for the future.

"We have a lot of work to do. We have a lot of missions. We're going back to the moon, and we're not going without Ohio," said Marcia Lindstrom, strategic communications manager for NASA's Space Launch System. Dr. Jimmy Kenyon, director of NASA Glenn Research Center, has stated Ohio is vital to the future of space travel.

"Now we can say that the road to the moon and Mars goes through Ohio," he said at the Ohio Space Forum in 2023. "It's not going to be an easy road. It's a big vision. It's going to take time to get there. We need to continue the momentum, continue the support. We need to continue driving forward. We need everybody on board. It's an exciting time to be in Ohio."

From the fiery crucible of combat in three theaters of war, to the silent expanse of space, John Glenn Jr. soared, charting a course of heroic exploration that inspired a nation and the world.

John Glenn

*Through the Skies to the Stars:
The Pioneering Spirit of the First American
to Orbit Earth*

Some people find themselves at the crossroads of history. John Herschel Glenn Jr. found himself there many times during his life. Though he believed in fate, he also acknowledged people have a hand in it.

"My view is that to sit back and let fate play its hand out and never influence it is not the way man was meant to operate," Glenn said during a press conference. He worked to influence his fate throughout his life.

Glenn was born July 18, 1921, in Cambridge, Ohio. He first flew on an airplane at 8 years old.

One day, while his father was driving, they saw a biplane flying overhead. Looking at the boy, who was enraptured by the sight, John Glenn Sr. asked his son if he wanted to go up. The answer would echo throughout history: "Yes." His father, a war veteran, soon took his young son for his first plane ride.

"I always had an interest in flying ever since I was a little kid, and I remember riding along with my dad in the car or something, and I'd have one of these little airplanes with a little prop that would run," Glenn recalled during an interview at Johnson Space Center. "I'd hold it out the window and watch the prop run and things like that. ... I guess I was about six or seven years old when (Charles) Lindbergh's flight occurred, and I still remember that as being an area of great interest around the community ... as far as influencing me."

Glenn recalled building model airplanes as a kid, carving them out of old balsa wood.

"So, I always had a lot of interest in aviation, but I never really thought in those days that I'd be able to fly myself, because flying was pretty expensive," he stated. The idea of flight stayed with Glenn, however, as he grew.

Glenn graduated from New Concord High School and studied chemistry at Muskingum College.

"What happened was, when I was in college, this was just prior to World War II, and the government had started a program called Civilian Pilot Training (CPT) and you could take flight training in little light planes," Glenn stated. "The one I learned to fly in was a ... 65-horsepower Taylorcraft with a Lycoming engine on it. I still remember that."

In 1941, Glenn earned his private pilot's license. He would quit college to enlist in the U.S. Army Air Corps in 1942. During his advanced flight training he was offered to transfer to the U.S. Marine Corps, which he did. Glenn served as part of the garrison on Midway Atoll on Feb. 21, 1944. He also flew fifty-seven combat missions around the Marshall Islands in 1944. During his military service for World War II, he received two Distinguished Flying Crosses, ten Air Medals, World War II Victory Medal, American Campaign Medal, Asiatic-Pacific Campaign Medal, Navy Occupation Service Medal, and the China Service Medal.

"I came back from World War II, and I liked flying," he remarked. "We were flying the old Corsairs, the old, converted gull-wing airplane that is still pretty famous, even to this day. I had more flight time in that than anything I ever flew.... I came back from World War II then, and decided I wanted to keep on flying. I liked it, loved it, and I was good at it. I won't be humble about that. I was good at it."

Glenn returned to the United States in February 1945, where he became captain and qualified for a regular commission. In 1945, he volunteered for service in northern China, flying patrol missions. He returned to the United States in 1948 and became a student at the Naval School of All-Weather Flight, before becoming a flight instructor. He also took courses at the Amphibious Warfare School and had jet training. He became a major in 1952.

In October 1952, Glenn was ordered to go to South Korea during the Korean Conflict. In 1953, he asked for an inter-service exchange position with the U.S. Air Force. Glenn would fly sixty-three combat missions in Korea. He said Korea was his first real air-to-air combat, and he was doing it in jets. He would fly low during close air-support missions and take a barrage of hits from ground fire. A couple of times he returned to base with more than 250 holes in his plane.

John Glenn

While in Korea, Glenn flew with baseball great Ted Williams as his wingman. Williams later told the Chicago Tribune that Glenn was "absolutely fearless. The best I ever saw. It was an honor to fly with him."

Glenn also praised Williams, stating, "He gave flying the same perfectionist's attention he gave to his hitting." After Williams' death in 2002, Glenn said, "Ted may have batted .400 for the Red Sox, but he hit a thousand as a U.S. Marine.

"Ted was a great wingman, though he didn't like to fly on instruments," Glenn reflected. "He took two hits during the war and was lucky to survive." One of those times, Williams refused to eject from the cockpit and landed his plane while it was on fire.

"He was a dedicated American and a terrific pilot," Glenn stated. The friendship between Glenn and Williams would last decades. It was detailed in the book, The Wingmen by Adam Lazarus.

Glenn called the Korean War "a unique time in fighter aircraft history," and stated:

"It was so much faster, because if you have an airplane coming toward you at 550 or 600 miles an hour and you're doing the same thing toward him, you're closing at 1,000 miles an hour and your decision-making and your maneuvering have to be really accelerated on a speeded-up basis," he stated. "But you're not using the kinds of weapons systems we have now. We didn't have radar to pick people up. It was all visual. And you had six .50-caliber machine guns mounted on your airplane, and you had to maneuver in behind the other airplane and get in to within about 800 to 1,00 feet with him maneuvering, too, and draw a lead on him. It was that kind of flying, at jet speeds with World War I-type tactics, basically."

While in Korea, Glenn earned the Navy Unit Commendation for Service, Korean Service Medal, and more honors. Before leaving, Glenn wrote a letter to request an assignment to fight test training. He was accepted.

"I lucked into that, too, because it was a good time because it was the first of the Navy and Marine supersonic fighters and attack aircraft that were just being tested, and that's when I hit Patuxent (Patuxent River Naval Air Station)," Glenn disclosed. "So, it was a great time to be there."

After four years doing flight test work, Glenn was assigned to what was then the Navy Bureau of Aeronautics in Washington as a project officer. During his time with the bureau, Glenn set the transcontinental speed record, traveling from Los Angeles to New York in 3 hours and 23 minutes. His flight in July 1957 in a F-8U Crusader was the first transcontinental flight to average supersonic speed.

The National Advisory Committee for Aeronautics (NACA), the precursor to the National Aeronautics and Space Administration (NASA), then asked for a test pilot from the Navy Bureau of Aeronautics to visit Langley Air Force Base and make runs on space flight simulators to test different re-entry shapes for crafts. There would also be G-force testing in a centrifuge. Glenn volunteered. Through his work, he helped design the Mercury Space Capsule, acting as a service advisor. He then heard that the military was looking for astronauts and "immediately volunteered."

"I thought it was a natural extension of the test pilot work I'd been doing, and sounded like it would be fascinating," he reflected. "So it was mainly because of that background, then, the immediate background, that I thought it was a natural step right on to the astronaut work."

The U.S. military selected the first astronauts in 1959, using the criteria that the men selected had to be military personnel with jet aircraft experience and backgrounds in engineering. Physically, the men had to be shorter than 5 feet 11 inches tall, which was the height needed to fit into the Mercury spacecraft. Glenn just barely made the height requirement, standing at 5 feet 10 ½ inches tall. Candidates also had to pass myriad other physical and psychological tests.
Glenn was one of more than 100 men who were examined for the program. The physical tests weeded the number of candidates down to just seven.

While waiting to hear if he was selected, Glenn return to the Navy Bureau of Aeronautics. He soon received a phone call from Charles Donlan, the associate director of Project Mercury, telling him he had been selected.

"Once we were selected and started into this whole training program, it was sort of open-ended as to what kind of things people could think up for us to do that might have some weird, remote application to space flight, and we had some pretty good ones that people thought up," Glenn pointed out.

Part of that was G-force training, with the force being taken onto the chest because astronauts would be lying down during takeoff. G force means gravitational force equivalent, which in basic terms means a perception of weight. For example, simply standing on Earth is equivalent to 1G. G forces can be positive (which make you feel heavier, like going uphill on a roller coaster) and negative (giving the feeling you are falling up, like going downhill on a roller coaster). Both positive and negative G Force can physically affect people. Positive G force can cause increased heart rate, blood pressure, and breathing, and redout (blood pooling in the head). Negative G force can cause loss of vision. Both can cause people to lose consciousness.

Astronauts must withstand both positive and negative G forces during a spaceflight from launch (positive G force) to re-entry into Earth's atmosphere and landing (negative G force). Astronauts have anti-G suits that help apply pressure to stop blood from pooling in their heads and perform maneuvers to push blood back into their heads when dealing with negative G forces. The G-force tests helped astronauts train to withstand these forces to ensure safe travel to and from space.

"I remember at seven G's was about as high as you could go and still get your ... arms [up]," he stated. "I remember we were trying to define ... at what G level you could still reach up to change a switch or something on the instrument panel, and seven G's was about the most — you couldn't lift your arm out of the couch, no matter how hard you tried, you couldn't lift your arm out of the couch above six or seven G's."

Mercury flights were expected to reach around 8 G's.

There were other centrifuge tests as well. One, which involved both Glenn and Alan Shephard, dealt with what would happen if an emergency re-entry had to be made on land.

"Those were really tough runs we did on the centrifuge," Glenn said. "What we did was set up our restraint system to see whether it was adequate .... [What] we wanted to do was simulate G's where you were coming out of the couch and hitting the restraints."

The action would make the capsule rotate from positive to negative G's. Flight surgeon William Augerson did the runs too. Glenn and Shepard got up to four G (positive) to four G (negative) while Augerson hit five and five, but with issues.

"He came out of it at the end of the thing, he was breathless and was coughing and couldn't seem to catch his breath," Glenn said. They decided to stop for a while. They discovered that two things had happened: Augerson had alveolar compaction, and the tiny blood vessels under the skin where the straps hit had ruptured. An anthropomorphic dummy was run through the centrifuge as well and they found that at five G's, the heart had swung around behind a lung to knock the air out of it.

"And so we decided at that point—the doctors and Al and I decided together—that was about enough of that experiment," Glenn declared.

Another experiment involved a "runaway' spacecraft with an uncontrollable rotational speed. A Multi-Axis Space Training Inertial Facility (MASTIF) was set up with a simulated cockpit to train astronauts to handle the craft when it would pitch, roll, and yaw going up to 30 revolutions per minute.

"You're in there looking at the rate instruments trying to control this thing down and it was the original vomit machine, I'll tell you," Glenn recalled. "That was a gut-buster. .... But the only time that [training] was ever used was, I think Neil Armstrong on the Agena."

In addition to the flight training, Glenn and the other Mercury astronauts were given special assignments to ensure pilot input in the development of future spacecraft. Glenn worked on cockpit layout and control functioning.

Project Mercury would send its first astronaut into space on May 5, 1961, when Shepard piloted Mercury's Freedom 7. The flight only lasted a little over fifteen minutes and was designed to determine humankind's capabilities in space and be able to safely return to Earth. Next up would be Virgil Grissom on the Liberty Bell 7, which would continue to study man's capabilities in space. Grissom's flight launched on July 21, 1961, and again lasted a little more than 15 minutes. Glenn served as backup crew for Grissom.

Glenn's flight was the third in the Mercury program and would last much longer than the other two. He would orbit the Earth three times, his flight lasting almost 5 hours. The mission would place Glenn in the history books as the first American in orbit.

In John Glenn: A Memoir by Glenn and Nick Taylor, Glenn stated that he wanted his kids, John David and Carolyn Ann, to feel part of his mission, and asked them to think of a name for his spacecraft. There was only one real rule.

"The world is going to be watching, so the name should represent our country and the way we feel about the rest of the world," Glenn told them. The duo came up with a list that included: hope, harmony, kindness, endeavour, Magellan, and Columbia, but at the top of the list was friendship.

"I was so proud of them," Glenn beamed. "They had chosen perfectly."

On January 27, 1962, Glenn was prepared to orbit the Earth. However, the weather had different ideas. The flight, in fact, would be delayed 10 times due to various issues ranging from weather to equipment delays.

Finally on Feb. 20, 1962, Friendship 7 launched. As Glenn took off, fellow astronaut and mission controller Scott Carpenter uttered "Godspeed, John Glenn." Though Glenn did not hear the sentiment as he blasted off into space, it struck a chord across the nation.

Radioing back to Mission Control during his flight Glenn would state, "I am go. The capsule is in good shape. All systems are go ... The view is tremendous ... beautiful."

The spacecraft made it into orbit. Glenn had experienced approximately 7.7 Gs during his orbital flight. While things had gotten off to a good start, the vessel ran into an issue near the end of its first orbit around Earth. The automatic control system wasn't functioning correctly. Glenn had to go to manual control, which he continued through the second and third orbits.

There also was a faulty switch in the head shield circuit that claimed the clamp holding the shield was released. Though the alert wasn't true, a retropack was kept in place to make sure the shield was steady.

Glenn researched spectrographic work during his orbital flight but said "the main purpose of my flight was to find out what reaction the human body had to extended weightlessness. Some of the doctors, for instance, before the flight thought that my vision might change during flight, because when the eye no longer had to be supported by the structure under the eye, it might gradually change shape, and if it did, you might get horribly myopic or something where you couldn't see properly," he explained. There also were concerns about "uncontrollable nausea and vertigo" because of changes to fluids in the inner ear.

"So, the eyes were one thing I was to check," Glenn stated. "Whether I felt any imbalance or vertigo was another thing to be checked. They didn't know whether you could swallow properly or not. I wasn't going to be up long enough that I really had to have a meal or two meals or anything, but they wanted me to take material along to swallow, which I did. They wanted to know if there was any change of feel, fingers or anything like that, any tendency toward any sickness, whether it was induced from the inner ear or whatever. It was more to find out the body's reaction to flight so we'd know whether we had to make any adaptation before we could go on to longer flights or to the flights that would later build up to go to the moon."

Glenn's nearly five-hour flight in orbit soon came to an end. During re-entry, portions of the retroback flew by Glenn's window, but the aerodynamic force on the vessel was strong enough then to hold the shield in place. Friendship 7 would touch down in the Atlantic Ocean about 800 miles from Cape Canaveral.

Glenn and Friendship 7 were picked up 21 minutes after landing by the USS Nova. Crews on the destroyer had spotted the main parachute of the space vessel and moved to rendezvous. Glenn was taken to a special hospital on Grand Turk Island to make sure he was in good shape. He then underwent debriefing. Dr. William Douglas of the astronaut team later declared that Glenn's health indicated that "anybody from 6 to 60 could ride as a passenger" and withstand the stresses of an hours-long trek into space.

Glenn's entire flight had been closely monitored by the world. Children throughout the United States followed Friendship 7's launch and re-entry on television sets in classrooms. Hospitals even wheeled televisions or radios onto each floor to make sure people could see the first American in orbit. His return to Cape Canaveral also garnered a lot of media attention.

"Glenn was greeted by the cheers and handclaps of his countrymen — and a host of kids who ducked and darted around adults for a glimpse of their space hero," the Associated Press reported.

It was at Cape Canaveral that President John F. Kennedy presented Glenn with the Distinguished Service Medal on Feb. 23, 1962. More important to Glenn, however, was seeing his family, whom he hugged and kissed as soon as he landed. He made sure to return a small gold lapel pin to his wife that he had carried on his flight. Kennedy gave a short speech as well, telling Glenn that the medal he was bestowed was for Glenn's courage and "outstanding contribution to the human knowledge." Kennedy even joked as he brought Glenn's family on stage, pointing out Glenn's mother and introducing her as "Mrs. Glenn, who launched Col. Glenn originally."

While Glenn's flight unified the nation, it also had international repercussions. Vice President Lyndon B. Johnson spoke during the ceremony to welcome Glenn back to Cape Canaveral, telling the crowd that President Dwight D. Eisenhower and Kennedy had both proposed to the world to have a "peaceful, joint exploration of space," however it had not been received as well as they had hoped.

"This stalwart Marine, John Glenn, was the first to bring from Premier Khrushchev of Russia a proposal that we attempt to explore space jointly — and that is something two presidents were unable to do. Welcome aboard," Johnson stated.

"I'm glad to be aboard," Glenn replied. "I'm very proud of my flight."

Glenn went on to thank the whole team of people who were involved in Project Mercury, stating that he was receiving acclaim only as a representative for all those who had made the flight possible. He also added that Mercury was only the "first step" in a long program. Later, Glenn was treated to celebrations in Washington, D.C., and a ticker-tape parade in New York. Then, Glenn and Friendship 7 went on a world tour. After the tour, Glenn wanted to return to space on one of the next flights. Unfortunately, he would have an extremely long wait.

"After my flight, I wanted to get back in rotation and go up again," he stressed. "Bob Filruth, who was running the program at the time, said that he wanted me to go into some areas of management of training and so on, and I said I didn't want to do that. I wanted to get back in line again for another flight. But he said headquarters (Washington, D.C.) wanted it that way, at least for a while. And I didn't know what the reason was, and I kept going back [to ask]."

Every time he did, Glenn was told the same thing: Washington didn't want him to go back to space yet.

John Glenn

Glenn had no idea at the time that he was seen as "too valuable" to risk on another space mission. The first American in orbit was given 'national hero' status, and there were political risks associated with allowing another flight. President Kennedy made the decision that he didn't want Glenn used again right away.

"If I'd known as much about Washington operations as I know now, I'd have gone to Washington and talked to somebody, but I didn't know that much then," Glenn stated in 1997. "So I accepted that for what it was, and this went on for the better part of two years. So I finally decided I'd go on and do other things, because I didn't want to stick around forever."

Glenn resigned as an astronaut on Jan. 16, 1964. A year later, he would retire from the U.S. Marine Corps and begin to take an active part in politics and environmental protection efforts. The want to return to space never truly left him. During his time at NASA, he earned the United Nations Service Medal, Navy's Astronaut Wings, and the Marine Corps' Astronaut Medal.

In 1964, he announced his intention to run for the Democratic nomination for the Senate in Ohio. However, a head injury Glenn sustained at his home gave him a concussion and caused persistent dizziness, nausea, and a ringing noise in his ears. Doctors barred him from campaigning. He later withdrew from the campaign to devote time to his recovery. In 1968, Glenn went on the campaign trail with his friend Sen. Robert Kennedy who was seeking the Democratic presidential nomination.

Glenn was at the campaign event when Robert Kennedy was shot by Sirhan Sirhan in the kitchen at the Ambassador Hotel in Los Angeles. Robert Kennedy was taken to the hospital for surgery and his wife, Ethel, asked the Glenns to take the Kennedy children home to Virginia.
Glenn and one of the Kennedy's neighbors would be the ones to tell the Kennedy children of their father's death.

Glenn decided to run for the Democratic nomination for the Senate again in 1970. However, the Ohio Democratic Party and major labor unions already were backing Howard Metzenbaum. Glenn's campaign was considered unorganized and underfunded, something he kept in mind for future campaigns. Though he lost the nomination, Glenn was appointed as chairman of the Citizens Task Force on Environmental Protection for Ohio.

In 1974, Glenn returned to run for the Democratic nomination for Senate. He would again face Metzenbaum. Glenn was better organized, but Metzenbaum still had the backing of the Ohio Democratic Party. Metzenbaum, however, stated during a debate that Glenn never really held a job. Glenn took that as an insult not just to him, but to any member of the military. In what became known as the "Gold Star

Mother Speech" during a debate at the Cleveland City Club, Glenn answered that insult. Glenn stated he spent 23 years in the U.S. Marine Corps and was in two wars. He reminded Metzenbaum and the crowd that he was in the space program.

"It wasn't my checkbook it was my life on the line," Glenn firmly stated. "It was not a nine-to-five job where I took time off to take the daily cash receipts to the bank. I ask you to go with me, as I went the other day, to a veterans' hospital and look at those men, with their mangled bodies, in the eye and tell them they didn't hold a job. You go with me to any Gold-Star Mother and you look her in the eye and tell her that her son did not hold a job.

"You go with me to the space program, and go as I have gone, to the widows and orphans of Ed White and Gus Grissom and Roger Chaffee, and you look those kids in the eye and tell them that their dad didn't hold a job. You go with me on Memorial Day coming up and you stand in Arlington National Cemetery, where I have more friends than I'd like to remember, and you watch those waving flags. You stand there, and you think about this nation, and you tell me that those people didn't have a job."

The speech was devastating to Metzenbaum's campaign. Glenn would win the primary election by nearly 100,000 votes. He then won the general election and became a U.S. Senator.
Glenn would serve on the Government Operations Committee, Interior and Insular Affairs Committee, Energy Research and Water Resources Subcommittee, and chaired the Energy, Nuclear Proliferation, and Federal Services Subcommittee. He worked to address the energy crisis of the 1970s, as well as introduce legislation to stop the spread of nuclear weapons. He worked on the nuclear weapons issue for the entirety of his Senate career.

Glenn spent four consecutive six-year terms in the Ohio Senate — more than any previous Ohio senator. In 1984, he ran for the Democratic nomination for president, but dropped out after Super Tuesday.

During his time as Senator, Glenn would be a member of the Senate Foreign Relations Committee, chairman of the East Asian and Pacific Affairs subcommittee and helped introduce legislation that forms the foundation of U.S.-Taiwanese foreign relations. His expertise in science and technology was utilized several times. He would become the chairman of the Government Affairs Committee, worked on the Senate Foreign Relations Committee, Senate Armed Services Committee, and many more.

In 1989, Glenn was caught up in what became known as the "Keating Five Scandal." Charles Keating, a former campaign contributor to Glenn, asked Glenn to meet with officials from the Federal Home Loan Bank board about delays in the board's audit of Lincoln Savings and Loan. Glenn and other senators attended meetings with the board. Glenn found out that the audit may lead to criminal charges against bank officials. He left the meetings and refused further involvement. Two years later, Lincoln Savings went bankrupt, and the meetings were seen as possible evidence of corruption. Glenn and the other four senators were investigated by the Ethics Committee. In the end, the committee stated that Glenn had used poor judgment but did nothing wrong.

Glenn would win his fourth Senate term and ended up representing Ohio for 25 years. In 1997, Glenn announced he would not seek a fifth Senate term. He retired in December 1998, but before he did, he took one more trip to space. It was something Glenn had been pushing toward for a long time.

"There are some things that have happened that I think are extremely interesting strictly from a research standpoint, whether it would be for me to go up or whether it be somebody else," Glenn reflected in 1997. "Things happen to astronauts in the normal 30- to 50-some age bracket when they go up now."

He pointed out that the body's immune system, cardiovascular system, and orthostatic tolerance changes. Things go back to normal, however, when astronauts return to Earth.

"Now what's the correlation?" Glenn asked. "Those same functions can be defined as things that happen to the older folks in our society just by the fact of growing older. ... Now, NIA, the National Institute of Aging, is interested in finding out that if you would send an older person up, would that person be more or less immune from the changes that the younger people go through, or would that be additive to what's already occurred?"

Glenn wondered what triggers the osteoporosis and cardiovascular changes.

"If you can find that out, for instance, maybe you'd have a whole new approach to cancer and disease and AIDS and problems with the elderly, as well as maybe problems with why the immune system changes for younger people in microgravity," he stated. "So, it's a whole new area and it's of interest. There are about 44 million Americans over the age of 60 right now. They're very interested in this."

On Jan. 16, 1998, NASA Administrator Dan Goldin appointed Glenn as a member of the Space Shuttle Discovery. Glenn was the subject of research on how weightlessness affects older individuals. Glenn was 77 when he returned to space.

"My age will not be the only difference from the first flight," Glenn stated in an article he wrote for The Elyria Chronicle Telegram's children's section called the

Mini-Page. "The inside of Discovery is more than 60 times larger than Friendship 7. That's a lot more room to move around in! Plus I will be flying with six other astronauts this time, and I will be in space for nine days, as opposed to just under five hours in my original flight.

"I do not think any of us realized how advanced the space program would become when we first began," he continued. "I believe someday, perhaps within your lifetime, space flight may become as common as flying across the county. You may even go into space, and perhaps explore farther than I did or will do. As long as you continue to study and work hard, I believe you can achieve anything."

Discovery launched Oct. 29, 1998. It had been thirty-six years, three months, and nine days since Glenn's Friendship 7 flight. Once again, crowds gathered to watch Glenn be launched into orbit. In New Concord, Ohio, approximately 2,000 people gathered including seniors and elementary school students at Muskingum College to watch the launch. After liftoff, students held a ceremony and buried a time capsule in front of the John Glenn Gymnasium on campus. Interestingly enough, Carpenter was again at Mission Control.

"Good luck to the crew," he radioed. "Safe flight. Godspeed, John Glenn."

Later, Carpenter would say he planned to say "Godspeed, Discovery" but had gotten caught up in the excitement of the moment.

The primary objectives of Discovery's mission were to conduct scientific experiments in the SPACEHAB, retrieve a Spartan free-flier, and work with the Hubble Space Telescope Orbiting Systems Test and Internal Extreme Ultraviolet Hitchhiker payload. Glenn's primary duties were with the SPACEHUB. He studied the way certain proteins were processed during weightlessness, looked at sleep patterns in space between himself and other crew members, and was in charge of the flight's videos and photographs. Glenn also took part in educational activities in a radio session to students.

Glenn conducted several interviews from space, including one with CBS News' Walter Cronkite, to whom he wished a happy birthday on Nov. 4, 1998. Cronkite asked Glenn: 36 years ago after his Friendship 7 flight, where did he think space travel would be in 1998?

"Well, Walter, I'd hoped we would be where we are today, but I hoped the space station would come along a little faster than it has. It will get here one of these days," Glenn remarked. "Discovery, the shuttle here, one of these days will be used for what it was originally designed for — to carry people and equipment back and forth to a permanently orbiting space station. That's where the science will get even better."

Glenn said he always wished the space program would be further than it is, but understood the budgetary constraints. In another 36 years, Glenn said he hoped man would be to Mars and return to the moon.

"There are so many areas you can get into that I think it's impossible to tell. There is no limit to what we can do," he replied.

Goldin also passed on a few messages to Glenn from space. The first was from Glenn's wife Annie, which simply was "you ain't going up again." Glenn laughed at that. Goldin also stated Glenn got him in trouble with his 86-year-old mother, who called him up and asked when she was going into space.

"If you think you are tenacious, I don't know how I'm going to tell her no," Goldin stated.

"Good for her. I'm glad she has that kind of attitude," Glenn urged. "I think people should be doing what they want to do and what they can do. ...I admire her spirit. That's great."

Glenn really stressed that the experiments he was taking part in were of great importance not only for older people on Earth but for the space program as well.

"There are some fifty-three changes that occur in the astronauts' bodies when they are up here [to the] the younger people, but they return back to normal when they return to Earth," he stated, adding about eight to ten of those changes are part of the natural process of aging. "I'm up here to see if we can learn more about what turns the body on and off in these particular areas, so we maybe — in the future — get away from cardiovascular problems or immune system changes or osteoporosis, balance coordination problems that plague people on the ground and plague the younger astronauts sometimes for a period when they are up here in space. If we can use these comparisons to learn what turns the body on and off in these particular areas then perhaps we can someday not only help the astronauts up here on longer missions sometimes to Mars or whatever, but somehow take away some of the frailties of old age on Earth. If that can come out of some of these opening experiments right now, that is a great area of research for the space program for the future."

Discovery touched down on Nov. 7, 1998. Glenn had reached the record books again, becoming the oldest man in space. It was a record that would not be broken until 2021, when Wally Funk went into space at 82 and later in 2022 by actor William Shatner at age 90.

After his second space trip, Glenn had plenty to do on Earth. In 1999, the Lewis Research Center was renamed the John H. Glenn Research Center in his honor. In

2000, he founded the John Glenn Institute for Public Service and Public Policy at The Ohio State University (OSU).

"To me, there is no greater calling," Glenn said during an interview with the Cincinnati Enquirer. "If I can inspire young people to dedicate themselves to the good of mankind, I've accomplished something."

Later, during a commencement address at OSU, Glenn stressed to students that "we are more fulfilled when we are involved in something bigger than ourselves."

In 2006, NASA awarded Glenn and thirty-seven other astronauts the Ambassador of Exploration Award. In 2011, Glenn, Armstrong, Buzz Aldrin, and Michael Collins were awarded the Congressional Gold Medal for Distinguished Astronauts. In 2012, Glenn received the Presidential Medal of Freedom.

"On the morning that John Glenn blasted off into space, America stood still," said President Barack Obama when presenting Glenn the medal. "For a half an hour, the phone stopped ringing at Chicago police headquarters. New York subway drivers offered a play-by-play account over the loudspeakers. President Kennedy interrupted a breakfast with congressional leaders to join 100 million TV viewers to hear the famous words 'Godspeed John Glenn.'

"The first American to orbit the Earth, John Glenn became a hero in every sense of the word, but he didn't stop there serving his country," Obama continued. "As a senator he found new ways to make a difference. And on his second trip into space at age 77, he defied the odds once again. He reminds everybody, don't tell him he's lived a historic life. He says, 'are living,' — don't put it into the past tense because he still has a lot of stuff going on."

Indeed, he did. Glenn spoke at the Welcome, Discovery ceremony when NASA delivered the space shuttle Discovery to the Smithsonian's National Air and Space Museum in 2012. In 2014, Glenn and his wife watched as their daughter christened the Mobile Landing Platform John Glenn, a U.S Navy Ship. In 2015, the John Glenn College of Public Affairs opened at The Ohio State University. The college got its start in 1998 as the John Glenn Institute for Public Policy and Management. Glenn continued flying his private plane until he was 90. In June 2016, he attended a ceremony where Port Columbus Airport was renamed John Glenn International Airport.

Less than six months later, Glenn was admitted to the hospital for an "undisclosed reason." In December 2016, Glenn died at The Ohio State University Wexner Medical Center.
Glenn was the last living Mercury astronaut prior to his death on Dec. 8, 2016. He was 95 years old.

John Glenn

"John Glenn is, and always will be, Ohio's ultimate hometown hero, and his passing today is an occasion for all of us to grieve," Ohio Gov. John Kasich said at Glenn's passing. "As we bow our heads and share our grief with his beloved wife, Annie, we must also turn to the skies, to salute his remarkable journeys and his long years of service to our state and nation."

President Obama called Glenn a friend and a pioneer, saying in a statement: "John spent his life breaking barriers, from defending our freedom as a decorated Marine Corps fighter pilot in World War II and Korea, to setting a transcontinental speed record, to becoming, at age 77, the oldest human to touch the stars. John always had the right stuff, inspiring generations of scientists, engineers, and astronauts who will take us to Mars and beyond — not just to visit, but to stay."

During his lifetime, Glenn did so much. It's hard to think of anyone who he would envy for their experiences, but there is one person. In 2012, he told the Associated Press that he did not envy other space explorers with "one big exception" — Neil Armstrong.

"To this day, he's the one person on Earth I'm truly, truly envious of," he stated.

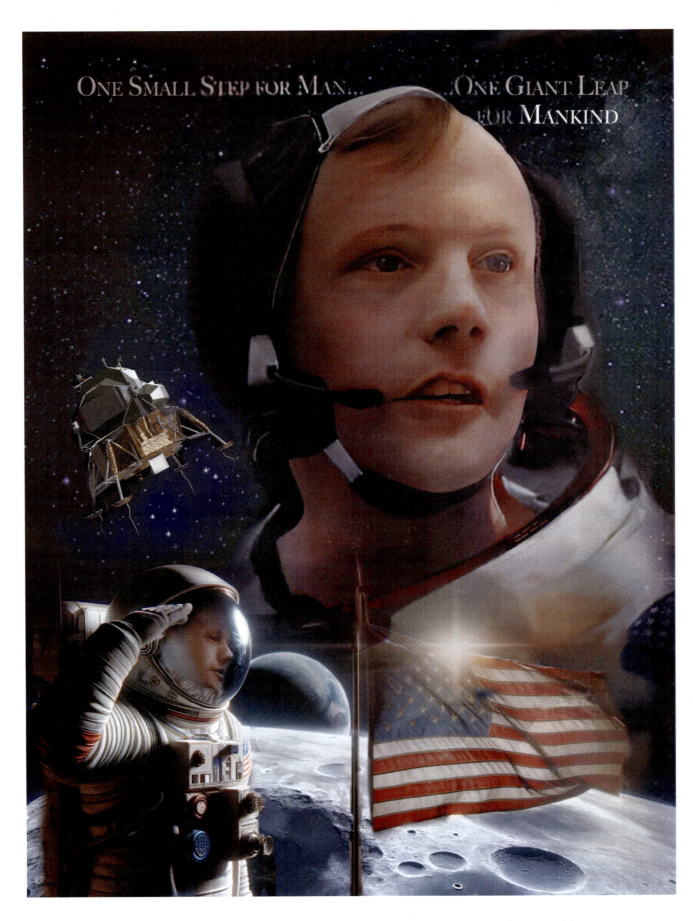

A Giant Leap: A historical moment of space exploration, reminding us of the monumental steps taken by astronauts on behalf of humanity.

Neil Armstrong

"That's one small step for man, one giant leap for mankind."

With those words, Ohioan Neil Armstrong captivated the world. Armstrong was born in Wapakoneta, Ohio, in 1930. His interest in flight was first sparked at the age of 2 after seeing the National Air Races in Cleveland. He had his first airplane ride at 6, taking flight in a Ford "Tin Goose" Tri-Motor in Warren, Ohio. Two years later, he had made up his mind about what he wanted to be.

"I began to focus on aviation probably at age 8 or 9, and inspired by what I'd read and seen about aviation and building model aircraft [is] why I determined at an early age … that was the field I wanted to go into," Armstrong recalled during an interview for the Johnson Space Center. At the time, he never could have guessed he would go to the moon. He wanted to be an airplane designer. "I later went into piloting because I thought a good designer ought to know the operational aspects of a plane," he recalled.

He started flying lessons at 15, earning money for lessons by taking various jobs in Wapakoneta as well as at the airport. A year later, he would have his student pilot's license. After high school, Armstrong received a Navy scholarship to Purdue University in 1947. He studied aeronautical engineering before being called to active duty with the U.S. Navy in 1949. Armstrong remembered receiving his aviation wings a year later.

"I got my wings in August of 1950, but that was about seventeen or eighteen months after I'd begun my active-duty service, so I still had another six months to go," he stated. "So I was one of those rare birds, a midshipman with wings. So I went to the fleet squadron, was in a standby unit for a while, then assigned to a jet fighter squadron [while I] was still a midshipman."

In 1950, Armstrong was sent to Korea. He flew combat missions during the Korean Conflict. During one mission, on Sept. 3, 1951, he had to eject from his plane.

"I actually ran through a cable, an anti-aircraft cable, and knocked off about six or eight feet of my right wing," Armstrong said. "If you're going fast, a cable will make a very good knife ... I was up maybe 500 feet or something, not an unusual altitude for the kind of things we were doing."

When he lost part of the wing, Armstrong radioed fellow pilot John Carpenter to decide whether to eject or try to land. With part of the wing missing, ejecting was the best option. He was able to steer the disabled plane into friendly territory before he "jumped out in the vicinity of Pohang Airport, 3, which was operated by U.S. Marines."

During the Korean Conflict, Armstrong would fly seventy-eight missions. He was awarded the Air Medal and two Gold Stars for his service. Armstrong's commission in the Navy ended in February 1952. He was released from active duty later that year. He had been placed in the Naval Reserves, however. He resigned from that commission in 1960.

After leaving Korea, Armstrong finished his Bachelor of Science degree in aeronautical engineering at Purdue. He then joined the National Advisory Committee for Aeronautics (NACA), predecessor to NASA. He worked at Lewis Flight Propulsion Center (now the Glenn Research Center). In 1955, he transferred to NACA's High-Speed Flight Station, which now bears his name.

At the station, he was very involved in the piloting and engineering aspects of the X-15 hypersonic rocket plane. Because of his engineering and technical abilities as a pilot, Armstrong was one of only twelve pilots to fly the North American X-15. Armstrong reached above Mach 5 (3,989 miles per hour) on three of his X-15 flights and reached a maximum altitude of 207,000 feet. Armstrong also had several other close calls during his X-15 work.

Milton Thomson, who was the chief engineer at Edwards, once spoke about when Armstrong was copiloting a B-29, from which a test rocket could be launched, when there was a runaway propeller. The propeller sliced through the bottom of the third engine, cut an oil line, severed flight control cables, and went into the lower fuselage. Armstrong and his fellow pilot managed to get the crippled plane back to the station.

There was also the time Armstrong's X-15 bounced off the atmosphere. According to reports he was "coasting out of fuel at three times the speed of sound" and overshot the landing site, ending up over the Rose Bowl in Pasadena. He managed to get back towards Edwards.

Despite the dangers, Armstrong loved being a test pilot. It was during a symposium for the Society of Experimental Test Pilots in October 1957 that Armstrong learned about Russia launching the first satellite into space — Sputnik.

"It did change our world," he said. "It absolutely changed our country's view of what was happening, the potential of space. I'm not sure how many people realized at that point, just where this would lead."

Armstrong also took part in the Boeing X20 Dyna-Soar program through the United States Air Force. The program began in October 1957, with Armstrong taking part from 1960-62. Its goal was to develop an aircraft that could travel at the speed of an intercontinental ballistic missile as well as reach Earth's orbit. It was to be used for reconnaissance, military applications, space rescue, and other missions.

NASA then announced it was accepting applications for the second group of astronauts to help with the Gemini and possibly the Apollo programs. The organization was looking for experienced test pilots who had flown high-performance jets and had earned engineering or physical/biological science degrees.

In 1962, Armstrong was selected by NASA for the second class of astronauts. He was one of nine men selected from 253 applications. Of those applications, one arrived a week after the June 1 deadline, but according to NASA, managers decided to accept it anyway. The late application was from Armstrong. The decision for him to apply for NASA "wasn't an easy" one.

"I was flying the X-15, and I had the understanding or belief that if I continued, I would be the chief pilot of that project," Armstrong reflected. "I was also working on the Dyna-Soar and that was still a paper airplane, but was a possibility. Then there was this other project down at Houston, [the] Apollo program. It wasn't clear to me which of those paths [would be best] ...

"I can't tell you now just why in the end I made the decision I did, but I consider it fortuitous that I happened to pick one that was a winning horse. But there would be no way to predict that at the time when it got to the fork in the road."

Though he questioned joining NASA, Armstrong soon became excited to be part of the program.

"It was going. It was happening. It was exciting," he exclaimed. "The goals, I thought, were important not just to the United States, but to society in general. I would have been happy doing anything they told me to do."

Some of Armstrong's responsibilities had proven, once again, to be a bit dangerous. His first "technical" NASA assignment was to monitor the development of mission simulators. He then served as the backup pilot for Gemini V. He became the prime command pilot for Gemini VIII, where he was the first U.S. civilian to fly in orbit.

Gemini VIII launched March 16, 1966. Flying with Armstrong was David Scott. The goal of the mission was to successfully dock with the Agena spacecraft that was in orbit. The two vessels docked together successfully, however once joined they started to roll. At first Scott and Armstrong thought the Agena was to blame. Scott used the docking adapter to send signals to the Agena control system, but nothing worked.

"When the rates [of revolution] became quite violent, I concluded that we couldn't continue, that we had to [separate from the Agena]," Armstrong recalled. "I was afraid we might lose consciousness because our spin rate had gotten pretty high, and I wanted to make sure that we got away [from Agena] before that happened."

Once detached, they found out it was Gemini's thruster that had the issue.

"We got serious problems here," Armstrong radioed to Mission Control during the flight. "We're tumbling end over end, and we've disengaged from the Agena." NASA calculated that Gemini VIII was spinning "at a rate of almost one revolution per second."

Armstrong was able to get the thruster under control, but the flight had to be cut short because of that issue.

"It was a great disappointment to us, to have to cut that flight short," Armstrong stated. "We had so many things we wanted to do, and I know Dave wanted to do an EVA (extravehicular activity) and try out the backpack and do all that kind of stuff. It was very disappointing to have to call it quits and come home."

Gemini VIII's flight only lasted 10 hours and 41 minutes. NASA then phased out the Gemini program and started Apollo. Unfortunately, that program began with tragedy. The Apollo 1 liftoff was set for Feb. 21, 1967, but would never happen. During a launch rehearsal at Cape Kennedy on Jan. 27, 1967, a spark ignited a fire that killed all three crew members — Gus Grissom, Ed White, and Roger Caffee. It would force NASA to suspend all Apollo missions for twenty months while hazards to the command module were handled.

For Armstrong, the fire meant the loss of friends in a way he could not fathom.

"I'd known Gus for a long time," he said. "Ed White and I bought some property together and split it. I built my house on one half of it and he built his house on the other. We were good friends, neighbors. [It was] some very traumatic times [after the fire]. You know, I suppose you're much more likely to accept the loss of a friend in flight, but it really hurts to lose them in a ground test. That was an indictment of ourselves. I mean [it happened] because we didn't do the right thing somehow. That's doubly, doubly traumatic."

The fire had started with an electrical spark. The combustible nylon material and high-pressure oxygen in the cabin enabled it to spread quickly. NASA officials delayed flights so the issues could be addressed — that meant the remaining astronauts had more time for training.

"We were given the gift of time," Armstrong reflected. "We didn't want that gift, but we were given months and months to not only fix the spacecraft, but rethink all our precious decisions, plans and strategies, and change a lot of things, hopefully for the better."

The Apollo program would start up again with Apollo 7 in 1968, though Armstrong was not involved in that flight. Armstrong was next assigned as the backup commander for the Apollo 9 mission. As part of that training, he conducted simulated lunar landings with the lunar landing research vehicle (LLRV-1) in Houston. One simulation ended in flames.

On Armstrong's 22nd flight of the test vehicle on May 6, 1968, something went wrong. He had been airborne for about five minutes when there was a loss of helium pressure in the vehicle that did not register on the LLRV's instruments. Armstrong lost control and had to eject less than 200 feet from the ground. The LLRV crashed and burned on impact. Armstrong was able to parachute to safety and was not harmed.

Engineers examined the vehicle and found the culprit in the helium pressure, discovering that the instruments had not registered the error to give adequate warnings. While the problems were corrected, another vehicle — the lunar landing training vehicle (LLTV) — was being used, as it had better structural integrity and electronics. Armstrong also trained on the LLTV, which he praised after his Apollo mission.

"It was a contrary machine, and a risky machine, but a very useful one," he said, adding he had "a good deal of confidence" flying the lunar module after training on the LLTV.

Armstrong's biggest challenge was yet to come as he was made commander of the Apollo 11 mission, the first mission to land on the moon. The crew included Armstrong, Michael Collins, and Edwin "Buzz" Aldrin Jr. They had six months to prepare for NASA's first lunar mission.

"Buzz Aldrin and myself [spent] a great deal of our time on mastering the lunar module, knowing it inside out and then we had, of course, to learn the experiments and the lunar surface all the different kinds of samples I could [take] as quickly and I could, stick them in the bag and get them back in the craft, and button up shop," he stated.

Collins stated that the crew "were all hard work, and we felt the weight of the world upon us."

During the mission, Armstrong and Aldrin went to the moon, while Collins circled overhead in the command module, the Columbia. Chris Kraft, NASA's director of flight operations in 1969, explained that Armstrong was the right choice to command Apollo 11.

"Neil was Neil — calm, quiet, and absolute confidence," he stated. "We all knew that he was the Lindbergh type. He had no ego. He was not of a mind that 'Hey, I'm going to be the first man on the moon.' That was never what Neil had in his head."

It may be for that reason, among others, that Armstrong was selected to be the first to set foot on the moon. Typically, the junior crew member would do spacewalks while commanders remained inside the module.

Apollo 11 launched on July 16, 1969. It not only carried Armstrong, Aldrin, and Collins, but also a bit of flight history. Armstrong's personal kit contained four pieces of the original muslin fabric and two pieces of the propeller from the Wright brothers' aircraft. Armstrong got the artifacts thanks to the U.S. Air Force Museum. On July 20, 1969, Apollo 11 landed on the moon.

"Houston, tranquility base here. The Eagle has landed," Armstrong stated. The mission had made history. Man had landed on the moon — traveling 240,000 miles from Earth. Despite landing on the lunar soil, it took several hours for Armstrong and Aldrin to leave the lunar module. It took longer to depressurize the module than anticipated as well as get the cooling units in the backpacks operating.

"When we actually descended the ladder it was found to be very much like the lunar gravity simulations we had performed here on Earth," Armstrong recalled. "No difficulty was encountered in descending the ladder. The last step was about three and a half feet from the surface, and we were somewhat concerned that we might have difficulty re-entering the (lunar module) at the end of our activity period."

Armstrong and Aldrin left the lunar module. As his foot stepped down on the lunar surface, Armstrong said his now famous quote: "That's one small step for man, one giant leap for mankind." The moment was short lived, however.

"It was special and memorable but it was only instantaneous because there was work to do," Armstrong later said. He would add that "the sights were simply magnificent, beyond any visual experience that I had ever been exposed to."

The two set up a TV camera, took photographs, collected lunar samples, spoke via telephone link to President Richard Nixon, and left behind commemorative medallions bearing the names of the three Apollo 1 astronauts who had died as well as the name of two cosmonauts who had perished. They also placed the U.S. flag on the moon. Armstrong and Aldrin would spend twenty-one hours and thirty-six minutes on the lunar landscape.

"It's a stark and strangely different place, but it looked friendly to me and it proved to be friendly," Armstrong said of the moon.

The mission was a success, though they did encounter a few bumps along the way. While trying to land, the crew experienced a "lumpy" lunar gravitational field. The landing site was riddled with boulders, and the fuel supply was diminishing. Armstrong was able to land — though the descent engine kicked up a lot of dust. They were 30 seconds from running out of fuel when the craft touched down on the moon.

"You got a bunch of guys down here about to turn blue," Charlie Duke in Mission Control said at the time.

After their historic moonwalk, the two returned to the lunar module to find a circuit breaker had broken off an instrument panel. Aldrin said in his book Magnificent Desolation: The Long Journey Home from the Moon that the circuit breaker needed to be pushed back in for the ascent engine to ignite in order for the astronauts to return home. The issue was reported back to Mission Control, however a solution to the broken switch wasn't forthcoming. Because the circuit was electrical, crews couldn't use anything metal or their fingers to push it into place. Eventually Aldrin would use a felt-tipped pen to fix the problem. With the circuit breaker in place, the lunar module returned to dock with Columbia. The trio of astronauts would return to Earth on July 24, 1969.

Upon landing back on Earth, the crew of Apollo 11 had to be quarantined because they had interacted with lunar material. There also was a desire to protect any potential life that may have been brought back. Armstrong would spend his 39th birthday in quarantine — but at least there was cake. On Aug. 5, 1969, staff at the Lunar Receiving Laboratory baked a cake for Armstrong. Twenty-one days after beginning quarantine, Armstrong, Collins, and Aldrin left the lab.

"I'd like to take this opportunity particularly to thank all of those of you I see out there who are my gracious hosts here at the Lunar Receiving Laboratory,"

Armstrong quipped. "I can't say that I would choose to spend a couple weeks like that, but I'm very glad that we got the opportunity to complete the mission."

Armstrong, Collins, and Aldrin were awarded the Presidential Medal of Freedom and later the Congressional Gold Medal for their lunar mission. They also received the NASA Distinguished Service Medal. The trio received a ticker tape parade in New York, Chicago, and Los Angeles. They then went on a 22-nation tour.

Armstrong, like Glenn, also went on to receive the Congressional Space Medal of Honor. He also was awarded the Cullum Geographical Medal from the American Geographical Society, Collier Trophy from the National Aeronautic Association, Dr. Robert H. Goddard Memorial Trophy from the National Space Club, Sylvanus Thayer Award by the U.S. Military Academy, Wright Brothers Memorial Trophy from the National Aeronautic Association, and more honors.

Despite going to the Moon and all his honors, Armstrong still had more things weighing on his mind — he had to pass an oral defense of his thesis at the University of Southern California for his master's degree. He passed.

Armstrong remained with NASA for several years after his historic flight, though he never went back into space. He acted as the deputy associate administrator for aeronautics at NASA. In 1970, he was part of the investigation into an explosion aboard Apollo 13, which caused it to abort its lunar landing. Unfortunately, it would not be the last investigation into an issue with a space vessel in which he would participate.

Armstrong resigned from NASA in 1971 and went on to teach in the Department of Aerospace Engineering at the University of Cincinnati. It was a position he would keep until 1979. Two years after Apollo 11, Armstrong spoke at the National Press Club, in one of his rare public appearances. He stressed the hard work of others in the space program. Of himself, Armstrong had this to say — "I am, and ever will be, a white-socks, pocket-protector, nerdy engineer."

In 1972, Armstrong's hometown of Wapakoneta dedicated its First on the Moon: Armstrong Air & Space Museum. The museum's goal continues to be to "inspire visitors to see themselves as tomorrow's explorers, able to solve problems in today's world" while providing "lifelong learning about the heritage of aviation and exploration of space, with an emphasis on the contributions of Neil Armstrong and other Ohioans."

Armstrong lived a fairly private life after leaving NASA. He never seemed to feel quite comfortable with his national hero status, however. As he told the Johnson Space Center in 2001, he felt as though working behind the scenes on the lunar flight should receive most of the credit.

"When you have hundreds of thousands of people all doing their job a little better than they have to, you get an improvement in performance," he said. "And that's the only reason we could have pulled this whole thing off." Armstrong admitted that many people think he stayed out of the public eye, but he didn't see it that way.

"I do so many things. I go to so many places. I give so many talks. I write so many papers that, from my point of view, it seems like I don't know how I could do more," he said. "But I recognize that from another perspective, outside, I'm only able to accept less than 1 percent of all the requests that come in, so to them it seems like I'm not doing anything."

He did continue to talk to children and others about the need for education and space travel.
Armstrong hosted an aviation history documentary from 1991-93 called "First Flights with Neil Armstrong." Armstrong interviewed pilots, engineers, and others as the documentary focused on technological aspects of aviation history.

In a 2005 interview with 60 Minutes, Armstrong stated he didn't feel like he should be famous.

"I just don't deserve it," he replied. "Circumstances put me into that particular role. That wasn't planned by anyone."

Meanwhile, Armstrong continued to fly aircraft in his free time. He flew until his 70s. In 1999, he and his Apollo 11 crewmates were awarded the Langley Gold Medal from the Smithsonian Institution. He was awarded the Naval Astronaut Badge in 2011 and received the 2013 General James E. Hill Lifetime Space Achievement Award. He was named to several halls of fame, including the International Space Hall of Fame and U.S. Astronaut Hall of Fame. The lunar crater where Apollo 11 landed and an asteroid bear his name.

Though Armstrong never returned to space, he was involved in various ways in the space program. On Jan. 28, 1986, Armstrong — like the rest of the nation — was struck by the tragedy of the Challenger Space Shuttle explosion, which killed the entire crew. President Ronald Reagan appointed the Rogers Commission to determine the cause. Armstrong was asked to serve as the vice chairman. Armstrong and another committee member, David Acheseon, were asked to write up the report. He also testified before Congress as the investigation into the disaster continued. It was not the last time he would speak before Congress on the space program.

In 2010, Armstrong was among the astronauts who spoke at a Senate hearing about the future of human spaceflight. He stressed the need to continue sending astronauts into space, adding that NASA would lose its edge if it did not.

"If the leadership we have acquired through our investments is simply allowed to fade away, other nations will surely step in where we have faltered," he stated. "I do not believe that would be in our best interest."

President Barack Obama planned to rely on private companies after the space shuttles retired. The president also had the goal to have humans land on asteroids and Mars. Armstrong, however, stressed there would be real benefits to returning to the moon. He stated that returning to the moon would allow individuals to train for "a lot of the things that you need to do when you are going farther out in the solar system" while maintaining close contact with Mission Control. While he stated that going to Mars was "a worthy challenge," he had concerns about the expense, time, and risks that had not been associated with the lunar program.

Armstrong died on Aug. 25, 2012. He was 82. At his passing, President Obama stated, "Neil was among the greatest of American heroes — not just of his time, but of all time. When he and his fellow crew members lifted off aboard Apollo 11 in 1969, they carried with them the aspirations of an entire nation."

Charles Bolden Jr., NASA's administrator at the time, said "as long as there are history books, Neil Armstrong will be included in them." He added Armstrong will be "remembered for taking humankind's first small step on a world beyond our own."

Armstrong donated his papers to Purdue University upon his death. In 2019, the university honored him when it launched its Neil Armstrong Distinguished Visiting Fellows Program to bring scholars and practitioners to the university to collaborate with faculty and students. After Armstrong's passing, the Dryden Flight Research Center was renamed the Neil A. Armstrong Flight Research Center in 2014. While that was an honor, Armstrong's family urged individuals to remember Armstrong with their actions.

"Honor his example of service, accomplishment, and modesty, and the next time you walk outside on a clear night and see the moon smiling down at you, think of Neil Armstrong, and give him a wink."

From Cleveland to the Cosmos: Charting the path from youthful dreams to the heights of space travel, navigating the thrill of success and the agony of impending disaster.

James Lovell

"Houston, we've had a problem."

These iconic words from Cleveland's own James Lovell mark a pivotal moment in space history, highlighting the inherent risks and the continual need for inventive solutions in mankind's journey to the cosmos. Lovell's life embodies this spirit of ingenuity.

Born just a year after Charles Lindbergh's historic transatlantic flight, Lovell was captivated by aviation from a young age. His childhood fascination with airplanes stayed with him through his formative years. In high school, Lovell's ambition to become a rocket engineer led him to reach out to the American Rocket Society (now the American Institute of Aeronautics and Astronauts) for guidance. Despite their advice to attend prestigious institutions like MIT or Caltech, financial constraints led him to chart a different course.

Embracing a pragmatic approach, Lovell secured a ROTC appointment, which paved his way to the Naval Academy. This was a stepping stone to his ultimate goal, as it led to flight training — his secondary interest. Lovell's academic journey saw him graduate from the United States Naval Academy with a Bachelor of Science degree in 1952, followed by stints at Test Pilot School and Aviation Safety School. His career as a test pilot spanned four years at the Naval Air Test Center in Maryland, and in 1971, he attended the advanced management program at Harvard Business School.

Lovell's astronaut journey began in 1958 when he was selected as a candidate for Project Mercury. However, a medical disqualification because of high bilirubin levels was a major setback, leaving him deeply disappointed but undeterred. His persistence paid off four years later when he successfully joined the astronaut program.

Though he entered during the Mercury era, Lovell's first assignment was in the Gemini program, serving as backup for the Gemini 4 flight. His notable space endeavors began with the Gemini 7 mission alongside Frank Borman in December 1965. This mission, aimed at evaluating new pressure suits and conducting various experiments, was historic for its nearly 14-day duration and successful rendezvous with Gemini 6, which was piloted by astronauts Wally Schirra and Thomas Stafford. It was a testament to human endurance and skill, demonstrating the feasibility of spacecraft meeting in orbit.

During this mission, Lovell's light-hearted message to Mission Control about his family's lawn needing mowing showcased his humanity amidst the challenges of space travel. The flight proved that it was possible to go to space for longer periods of time. The information was crucial, as NASA officials had previously thought a trip to the moon could last no longer than two weeks. The spacesuits, however, did prove a bit troublesome. Lovell called the suits "very hot, sweaty and bulky." NASA wanted at least one of the astronauts to have the suit on the whole time. Lovell couldn't stand it and said at one point, "I'm out of my suit. I'm in my underwear .... And, of course, my young son at the time said, 'Dad orbited the Earth in his underwear,' which is essentially what we did."

The mission was deemed a success. The next time Lovell went to space, it was onboard Gemini 12. Lovell commanded the flight. The mission was to end the Gemini program, while preparing for the Apollo program (which would take man to the moon).The flight launched in November 1966 with the goal of conducting spacewalks; using the Agena propulsion system to change orbit; using automatic re-entry; and conducting fourteen scientific, medical, and technical experiments. The flight lasted four days.

With the Gemini program complete, NASA began the Apollo program — but the flight of Apollo 1 never happened. A flash fire broke out on Apollo 1 during a simulation, killing all three astronauts inside. Lovell was among the astronauts assigned to panels to study what went wrong.

"We looked at how we can cope with in-flight emergencies — fires — to see what we'd have to have onboard or [what] we could do for it," he stated, adding it was a very "interesting investigation."

The Apollo program would continue with Lovell taking part in two missions. The first was Apollo 8, which was the maiden voyage to the moon in 1968. Lovell originally had served as a backup for the flight, but astronaut Mike Collins had a bone spur and couldn't go.

"You know, faith has sort of strange things because I never expected to be on Apollo 8," Lovell reflected. "But I have to tell you, that was the highpoint of my space career."

The flight would test the command and service modules, as well as demonstrate translunar injection, midcourse corrections, and other issues relating to lunar operations. Preparing for the flight, Lovell would examine surface charts of craters to get some idea of what he would be looking at when he went around the moon. Lovell would name a lunar mountain Mount Marilyn after his wife as he prepared for the Apollo 8 mission. The International Astronomical Union would eventually agree to the name in 2017. While it would take the union decades to agree to the name, astronauts used it quite a bit as it "took hold" in NASA.

"The Apollo 10 crew used it for their descent in testing the abortion phase of the flight," Lovell stated. "Apollo 11 used 'Mount Marilyn' as the point [where] they started to go into their landing site."

Just prior to the mission, Lovell would get to meet one of his heroes. Charles Lindbergh met with the Apollo 8's astronauts (Lovell, Borman, and William Anders) the night before the launch. The aviator was a fan of the space program and wanted to meet the men of the first lunar mission. The mission would not land on the surface but would be in lunar orbit.

Apollo 8 launched Dec. 21, 1968. The crew would spend Christmas in space, reading verses of Genesis to viewers during a telecast. Lovell would radio to Mission Control on Christmas, "Roger, please be informed there is a Santa Claus."

Apollo 8 entered lunar orbit during its mission — a big step toward landing on Earth's natural satellite.

"We were so curious, so excited about being at the moon that we were like three school kids looking into a candy store window, watching those ancient old craters go by — and we were only sixty miles above the surface," Lovell exclaimed. "I felt very, very honored and lucky to be there."

During the Apollo 8 mission, crew members witnessed the Earth coming up over the moon. Anders quickly asked Lovell for some color film to take a picture. Lovell was so excited about the beauty of what he was seeing, directing Anders to take several photos.

"Take several of them!" he exclaimed before becoming impatient and wanting to take the photos himself. "Here, give it to me."

"Calm down, Lovell," commanded Borman.

"Oh, that's a beautiful shot," Lovell exclaimed.

The photo would become known as "Earthrise," and it has been credited with starting the global environmental movement.

Apollo 8 landed safety at home and training immediately began for the first touchdown on the moon. Lovell was named the backup commander for Neil Armstrong during the Apollo 11 lunar mission. Lovell would remain on the ground as Armstrong would go on to be the first man on the moon. Lovell did, however, get to meet Lindbergh again, as he showed the aviator around prior to the Apollo 11 launch. Lovell reflected about how momentous the occasion was that Apollo 11 was going to the moon. Lindbergh said yes but had one caveat he thought the astronaut should know.

"Apollo 8 that first flight from the Earth to the moon — that's the flight I'll remember," Lindbergh stressed.

Lovell would be best known for his next mission, Apollo 13, which has been called "the successful failure." Apollo 13, with a crew of Lovell, Fred Haise, and Jack Swigert, launched on April 11, 1970. It was to be NASA's third moon-landing mission and the second time Lovell would travel to the moon.

While the flight lifted off fine, the center engine would shut down early after liftoff, however the remaining engines allowed the vessel to reach the proper orbit. Two days later, the crew would find themselves in a severely damaged spaceship approximately 200,000 miles from home. Lovell, who was the mission commander, recalled hearing a loud bang. He said during the test phase during training for the mission, Haise would make things bang so at first, he thought it was Haise.

"Then I looked up at him," Lovell stated. "I looked at him and his eyes were as wide as saucers ... Then, of course, things started to happen."

What was happening was, one of Apollo 13's oxygen tanks had exploded. Two of the three fuel cells were lost as well. Lovell decided to look out the window.

"I saw escaping at the rear of my spacecraft in sort of a flame or flume type of thing, a gaseous substance, and I realized quickly that the gas I saw coming out was oxygen," he revealed.

Swigert contacted Mission Control to tell them there was an issue, but they couldn't hear what he was saying. Lovell would utter the phrase, "Houston, we've had a problem."

NASA officials said "the resulting explosion plunged an entire nation into an anxious three-and-a-half day drama."

While crews on the ground scrambled to figure out what had happened and how to proceed, the three astronauts also were busy planning what to do. The explosion also had damaged the other oxygen tank and made using the fuel cells impossible.

"We were test pilots so had some training in the past," Lovell stated. "If you panic, where would you go? ... You had to say, 'OK what can we do to get home?' ... Individually, we all thought 'Holy cow what happens if we don't get home?'"

The crew had to enter "lifeboat mode" and use the lunar module Aquarius, which still had oxygen tanks. Crew members had to take the guidance parameters out of the command module and put them in the lunar model to find out their altitude during the continued flight. For three days, Apollo 13's crew dealt with shortage of water and electricity, dangerous levels of carbon monoxide, and falling temperatures (it would reach 38 degrees inside the craft). Engineers on Earth designed a method for getting hydroxide canisters from the command module to fit in the openings of Aquarius to remove the carbon monoxide to solve one issue.

The crews on Apollo 13 and Mission Control also had to figure out how to re-orient the lunar model to do a trajectory to return to Earth. Apollo 13 never entered the moon's orbit. Instead, the vessel swung around the moon — going over the far side of the moon about 158 miles from its surface — on what is called a "free return trajectory" to head back to Earth.

The crew also had to return to and power up the command module to come home. A command module had never been started from a full shut down in space before then. There was concern, however, if the cold condensation on the panel would cause a short when power was turned back on. Apollo crew members wiped the panel off with a towel. Thankfully, there were no problems, mostly because after the Apollo 1 fire a major redesign increased insulation to protect the wiring of the instrument panel.

The Apollo 13 command module would splash down in the Pacific Ocean on April 17, 1970. The recovery ship, the USS Iwo Jima, would pick up the three astronauts, who through their flight traveled the farthest distance from Earth reached by man (248,655 miles). It's a record they still hold to this day.

While Apollo 13 would make it home, Lovell would be the only man to ever travel to the moon twice but never set foot on it.

"It was frustrating and very disappointing at the time," Lovell recalled. "But over the years, I have come to the conclusion that the accident was the best thing that could have happened to NASA. It had become complacent after a stream of early Apollo successes. Suddenly, there was a potential catastrophe that brought out the fact spaceflight is inherently dangerous. It also highlighted the wonderful leadership and Mission Control team that we had. For those facts, it was a blessing in disguise."

When asked if he ever wanted to return to space following Apollo 13, Lovell recalled what happened during a press conference at Johnson Space Center after his return. NASA officials prior to Apollo 13 told other Apollo program crew members that if there was a problem on the flight, they would get them on another one. They never said that to Lovell, Haise, or Swigert prior Apollo 13 being launched. When a reporter asked Lovell if he was going to go for another mission, he thought he would say yes so NASA management could not back away from that promise.

"I was about ready to say something like that when out in the audience, I saw a hand go up," he laughed. It was his wife, who then gave him a thumbs down gesture. Lovell knew what he had to say then. "I said, 'No. I think this is the last flight I'm gonna make.'"

Though it would be his last time in space, Lovell held the record for the most time in space — 715 hours and 5 minutes — until that figure was surpassed by the Skylab flights.

In 1973, Lovell retired from the Navy and space program. He ended his astronaut career with many special honors and awards, including the Presidential Medal for Freedom, NASA Distinguished Service Medal, American Astronautical Society Flight Achievement Awards, Hubbard Medal, Institute of Navigation Award, and many others. Lovell would not be done with Apollo 13, however.

After recovering Apollo 13, NASA stored the vessel in a warehouse in Florida. Officials for Le Bourget Aerodome (where Lindbergh landed his plane after his non-stop trek across the Atlantic) in France then called and asked if NASA had any space artifacts they could put in Le Bourget's museum. NASA officials gave them Apollo 13. It remained there for twenty years. A friend of Lovell's wrote to him to let him know his spacecraft was in France. He and his wife decided to go see it.

"It was still on the cradle that they had rolled it in on," Lovell recalled. "It was all by itself, just about, nothing else around it. The hatch was missing. The instrument panel was missing. The seats were missing. The only thing I saw was a piece of paper that was stuck on the side that said 'Apollo 13,' and gave the names of the three crew members."

The three — Lovell, Haise and Swigert — had talked about writing about their experience on Apollo 13 when they sat on the recovery ship after the rescue. Nothing happened, however, until 1991, when journalist Jeffrey Kluger approached

Lovell about a book. Haise was not interested in taking part, and Swigert had died in 1982. The book became Lost Moon: The Perilous Voyage of Apollo 13. Director Ron Howard heard about it, even before the book was finished, and called Lovell to talk about the story.

The movie "Apollo 13" would open in 1995. Lovell would be portrayed by Tom Hanks. The movie would go on to win two Academy Awards and a Screen Actors Guild Award. Lovell would appear as the captain of the USS Iwo Jima, while his wife would be a spectator during the launch sequence in the movie. The movie also had an impact on the actual Apollo 13 vessel: The spacecraft was returned to the United States, going to the Cosmosphere museum in Kansas.

Today, Lovell continues to be an inspiration to many people, encouraging them to work to reach their dreams. As he once said, "There are people who make things happen. There are people who watch things happen, and there are people who wonder what happened. To be successful, you need to be a person who makes things happen."

Reflections of Endeavor: She honors the legacy of space shuttle missions and the enduring human spirit of exploration and discovery through intelligence and grit.

Judith Resnik

"In the silent vastness of space, astronauts like Judith Resnik knew that each leap towards the stars carries the shadow of risk. Her journey, blending engineering genius with bravery, embodies the astronaut's creed: the pursuit of discovery balances the bright light of success with the dark potential of sacrifice. At every launch, they stand at the threshold of both beginning and potential end, yet soar beyond fear, driven by the relentless spirit of human exploration."

Judith "J.R." Resnik could have been anything she set her mind to — and that included being one of the first women in space. A classical pianist, electrical engineer, biomedical engineer, pilot, and missile scientist, the Akron native had crafted quite a place for herself in the world, even before becoming an astronaut. Resnik became the first Jewish American and second American woman in space. She also helped create a device used for years on space shuttles.

Resnik majored in electrical engineering at Carnegie-Mellon (then Carnegie Tech). She then worked for RCA before earning her master's degree at the University of Maryland. She later earned her doctorate from the University of Maryland.

In 1974, Resnik became a biomedical engineer and staff fellow at the National Institutes of Health. For the next three years, she would perform biological research experiments, according to NASA. Before she was selected as an astronaut for NASA, Resnik already had performed some engineering support work for the agency with its sounding rocket and telemetry system programs. Working at RCA, she did research into integrated circuitry and worked on missile and radar projects for the military.

Interestingly enough, Resnik cited Star Trek's Nichelle Nichols (Lt. Uhura) for influencing her decision to apply at NASA. Nichols had led a promotional campaign to encourage women and minorities to apply to NASA in 1977-78. Later, in 1984, Resnik would deliver the citation for Nichols' Distinguished Civil Service Award.

Resnik said that Nichols personified "outstanding initiative, leadership, and accomplishment."

Resnik was selected as an astronaut candidate in 1978, one of six women chosen to become astronauts. She was eager to learn and eager to see the stars.
"I'd like to fly any mission. The intent of a mission specialist is to train us to be generalists and to learn a little bit about every field. ... I'd be glad to fly in anything they let me fly," Resnik beamed during an ABC World News Tonight interview in 1978.

Resnik was described as intelligent and friendly by many who knew her. Her personality was an added benefit, as her likeness was placed on a space mural by artist Robert McCall at the Johnson Space Center in the late 1970s. McCall said Resnik had breakfast with him a few times when he was working on the mural.

"So she joined me a couple of times, and I got to know her," he recalled. "So I painted her in that mural ... I put her name on the spacesuit, and I made it as close a likeness as I possibly could."

McCall said that while Astronauts John Young and Bob Crippen were also depicted on the mural, he ran into an issue with Resnik's image. McCall remembered receiving a call from headquarters and being told identifying "that female astronaut as Judy is bothering some" of the other new astronauts. It was strongly suggested that he take off the name.

"I made it so you can't read it," McCall said. "There is a name there, but only impressionistic. And also changed her features just a little bit. Well, I didn't do much. The hair is the same. But it is Judy, and to me it will always be Judy."

While Resnik preferred meeting with students to doing interviews with news organizations, her joy for the space program shined through in reports. Journalist Tom Brokaw asked Resnik in an April 1981 interview what the best part about being an astronaut was.

"Everything," she replied. Later, she talked about using her electrical engineering expertise in the space program.

"I think the best part technically is that it's a well-rounded approach to science and technology and we get to do a little bit of everything. It's state-of-the art and a challenge," she answered.

Resnik was assigned several projects to work on during her tenure at NASA. She worked on the Orbiter development, software, and the Remote Manipulator System (a robotic arm).

"Judy Resnik used to work with us quite a bit on the arm," said Sherwood "Woody" Springs, who worked on the Shuttle Avionics Integration Lab. Resnik had trained on the shuttle's robot arm since its inception. Her training would be a boon to NASA on her first space mission.

Resnik was selected to be part of the maiden crew on the Discovery Space Shuttle. The 1984 mission would last six days. Getting to space, again, took time. The first launch attempt on June 25, 1984, was delayed because of a computer issue. The next day, the launch was halted four seconds before liftoff once a fault was found in one of the main engines. Then on Aug. 29, 1984, another launch attempt was made, but that too was delayed for a day because of a software issue, according to NASA.

Finally, on Aug. 30, 1984, Discovery launched. Its mission included the deployment of three satellites as well as the solar array, which Resnik would deploy to test the structure. The solar array was, at the time, the largest structure ever deployed from a crewed space vessel.

"All in all it was a good flight test for large space structures with potential future use in either space-based construction or space station operations," Resnik explained during the post-flight press conference.

On the fifth day of the mission some ice formed on the side of the spacecraft. Commander Henry Hartsfield would use the RMS to dislodge the ice. Hartsfield praised Resnik for her work during that maneuver.

"Judy came up and handled the communications and kept me honest with the RMS — while we were doing this task — double checking the procedures," Hartsfield said during the post-flight press conference in 1984. Upon her return to Earth, Resnik would earn a NASA Space Flight Medal of Honor for her efforts on the Discovery mission.

Up in space, there also was another slight mishap that required Resnik to get a bit of a haircut.

"We have an IMAX camera up there, and we were doing some filming of the [satellite] launch," said astronaut Richard Mullane. He explained that Judy was floating between him and Hartsfield, who was filming with the camera. "... that IMAX camera has a belt-driven magazine, and Hank was filming [the satellite] as it moved away from the vehicle, and Judy — I don't know if you ever saw pictures of Judy — her hair, that long black hair of hers was just a wild riot around her head in weightlessness, and that belt-riven magazine sucked up a shank of her hair into that IMAX camera and jammed it."

Crew members cut Resnik's hair out of the camera, which popped a circuit breaker and caused the camera to stop.

"It looked like we might have destroyed the camera," Mullane detailed. "Mike [Coats] went down to the mid-deck and spent hours picking hair out of the gearing of that thing to make it so it could work again." It did work again, and clips from the mission were even used in the 1985 IMAX film "The Dream is Alive."

Discovery touched down on Sept. 5, 1984. Its mission was declared a success, however during a post-flight inspection, a problem was found. Soot was detected in the O-rings, rubber seals used in areas like the joints of rocket boosters. It was the first indication of a blow-by, when gasses penetrate the seal. That issue would lead to a tragedy two years later.

Immediately after Discovery, Resnik would start training for her next mission. She would be put on the roster to use the robotic arm again in 1986 as a mission specialist on the Challenger Space Shuttle. Joining the Challenger crew was Sharon McAuliffe, a teacher from New Hampshire, who was selected to take part in the NASA Teacher in Space program. She was to conduct lesson plans as well as act as a payload specialist on the mission.

The overall goals of the Challenger mission were to launch a second tracking and data relay system satellite, observe Halley's Comet, and conduct other experiments. Resnik would be primarily responsible for the deployment and retrieval of the satellites.

Challenger was set to launch on Jan. 27, 1986, but the launch was scratched because of a mechanical issue and then winds. On Jan. 28, 1986, the crew boarded Challenger for takeoff.
The nation had tuned into television to watch the launch, with many schools across the nation holding viewings to see the first teacher in space. Crowds, including many family members of the crew, gathered on the ground to watch the space shuttle head to the stars. It would never make it.

The Challenger broke apart following an explosion a little over a minute from liftoff. All seven crew members perished. A shocked country mourned. President Ronald Reagan spoke to the public that day in a nationwide address.

"Ladies and gentlemen, I'd planned to speak to you tonight to report on the state of the Union, but the events of earlier today have led me to change those plans," the president began. "Today is a day for mourning and remembering. Nancy and I are pained to the core by the tragedy of the shuttle Challenger. We know we share this pain with all of the people of our country. This is truly a national loss.

"Nineteen years ago, almost to the day, we lost three astronauts in a terrible accident on the ground. But we've never lost an astronaut in flight; we've never had a tragedy like this. And perhaps we've forgotten the courage it took for the crew of the shuttle. But they, the Challenger Seven, were aware of the dangers, but overcame them and did their jobs brilliantly. We mourn seven heroes: Michael Smith, Dick Scobee, Judith Resnik, Ronald McNair, Ellison Onizuka, Gregory Jarvis, and Christa McAuliffe. We mourn their loss as a nation together."

Resnik was 36 years old.

An inquiry began immediately following the Challenger disaster. A presidential commission, called the Rogers Commission, would oversee the investigation. Commission members included former U.S. Secretary of State and U.S. Attorney General William Rogers, astronauts Neil Armstrong and Sally Ride, former Chief Scientist of the U.S. Air Force Eugene Covert, Nobel Prize winner in physics Richard Feynman and several others. The commission would rule the cause of the Challenger disaster to be the failure of the O-ring seal, specifically on the aft field joint on the right-hand solid rocket monitor. The commission found that the "failure of the joint was due to a faulty design."

It also found "that NASA's drive to achieve a launch schedule of twenty-four flights per year created pressure throughout the agency that directly contributed to unsafe launch operations." It recommended NASA design a risk management program, provide crews with a means to escape during a control-guided flight, and that the shuttles' management structure, safety organizations, and maintenance policies needed to be improved. Other improvements also were suggested.

"Though we grieve at the loss of the Challenger crew, we do not believe that their sacrifice was in vain," the report stated. "They would not want us to stop reaching into the unknown. Instead, they would want us to learn from our mistakes, correct any problems that have been identified, and then once again reach out to expand the boundaries of our experience in living and working in outer space."

NASA went to work to address the issues — making several technical alterations to the shuttle and creating an office of safety, reliability, and quality assurance. It wouldn't be until 1988 that another space shuttle would launch.

Though her life was cut tragically short, Resnik left her mark on engineering, space, and the world. Following her passing, she has been honored in many ways. In January 1986, the Ohio Senate unanimously approved a resolution to honor Resnik. It reads, "Throughout her brief but prolific life, Judith Resnik exemplified the spirit which facilitates discovery in the universe and the true progress of humanity. [We] pay tribute to Judith Resnik's courage, dedication and faith which will undoubtedly live in the hearts of all that knew and loved her."

The Society of Women Engineers offer the Judith Resnik Memorial Scholarship to students majoring in aerospace, aeronautical, or astronautical engineering. The society also presents the Resnik Challenger Medal to women for their "visionary technical contributions to deep space and Earth-orbiting spacecraft; and for developing cost-saving, hardware-life-extending strategies that are making every bolder mission possible."

The Akron Community Foundation also honors her with a scholarship awarded annually to a female high school senior pursuing a career in math, science, or engineering. An elementary school in Maryland, dorm at Carnegie Mellon University, and many other facilities are named after her. Resnik, and the other Challenger astronauts, also were honored by the International Astronomical Union. In 1988, it approved naming a small lunar impact crater on the far side of the moon Resnik. Six other craters were named after the other Challenger crew members. In 1986, the Soviet Union named a crater on Venus after her. In 2004, Resnik and her fellow Challenger crew members received the Congressional Space Medal of Honor.

The Star Trek franchise also honored Challenger by dedicating Star Trek IV to the crew, stating, "The cast and crew of Star Trek wish to dedicate this film to the men and women of the spaceship Challenger whose courageous spirit shall live to the 23rd century and beyond..." The franchise also would mention Resnik in other ways — showing a starship named the USS Resnik and her mission patch in another movie.

In 2015, Resnik's niece, Jenna, shared with the Challenger Center, a nonprofit STEM education organization, what Challenger and her aunt's life experiences have taught her about the world. She urged people not to let what others think get in their way, and to work for their destiny like her aunt did. She closed with a quote from Resnik.

"It is very important for you to realize that people who you consider to be heroes are really quite like yourselves," Resnik had said. "Only hard work and perseverance will help you to succeed at any venture — there is no magic of being more 'special' than someone else."

Echoes of Exploration: The most famous non astronaut in the pantheon of spacemen.

Eugene Kranz

*"Gene Kranz was the unseen hero —
the backbone of U.S. space exploration —
steering success from Mission Control."*

You don't need to be an astronaut to be a space hero. Eugene "Gene" Kranz is an American hero who led by example through some of the space program's darkest days.

For Kranz, failure was not an option. Despite never going into space, in 2010 he was ranked second most popular space hero in an informal survey by the Space Foundation. Neil Armstrong was the only one to surpass him.

Kranz was born Aug. 17, 1933, in Toledo, Ohio. He always had an interest in aeronautics. In fact, while at Toledo Central Catholic High School he wrote a thesis discussing the possibilities of flying a single-stage rocket to the moon.

He graduated from St. Louis University's Parks College with a Bachelor of Science degree in aeronautical engineering. He then went into the Air Force Reserve, where he was commissioned as a second lieutenant. He received his wings before being sent to South Korea to fly patrols around the demilitarized zone. Coming back from Korea, Kranz went to work for McDonnell Aircraft Corporation, helping test and research missiles for the Air Force.

"After I came back from Korea, I became a civilian flight test engineer in the B-52," Kranz stated during an interview with the American Veterans Center. He said basically he was given the B-52 to develop technologies and systems "to allow that aircraft to penetrate Soviet airspace." He worked with a large group of people on the project, which had a lot of constraints.

"It was making risk-based decisions," Kranz explained. "Is it safe to fly this flight with the open items we have?"

In 1972, Kranz was discharged from the Air Force Reserves, having reached the rank of captain. With his B-52 project completed, Kranz needed to find another job. He had several opportunities, but an ad in Aviation Week magazine caught his attention.

"This said they're forming a space task group and looking for qualified engineers to determine the feasibility of putting an American in space," he told the Johnson Space Center's Oral History Project. "That sounds like a pretty interesting thing. I put in an application and didn't hear anything for a few weeks. ... Then I got a phone call."

Kranz was offered the job without ever having been interviewed. Later, he was tapped by flight director Christopher Kraft to be a Mission Control procedures officer.

"[Kraft] said 'I want you to go down to the Cape, write a countdown, write some mission rules, and when you're through give me a call and we'll launch.' That was the first Redstone launch," Kranz recalled.

The Mercury-Redstone test project involved unmanned vessels. Kranz has referred to the first Redstone launch as the "four-inch flight," as the rocket shut itself down and went back onto the pad after liftoff. It had only reached about four inches on its flight. The error was caused by two electrical cables — a control and a power cable — that separated in the wrong order.

"My first launch wasn't too swift," Kranz joked.

Kranz continued to work hard, then heard that Kraft was looking for people to be part of what was then called Mercury Control (now Mission Control). Kranz decided to be the person who provided Kraft's "voice out to the Mercury network."

"Most of the work we did in communicating was through teletype messaging," he explained. "Paper would be torn off and handed to a controller, the controller would read it to say, 'I wonder what he needs me to do.' I was gluing that thing together for Kraft," Kranz stated. "That was something he needed to do because he had to worry about spacecraft, the crew, those kinds of things. I made sure all the functions necessary to support the mission were operating."

Kranz also wrote the go/no go procedures that were used to determine if missions were to continue as planned or be aborted. He worked as a procedures officer for all the crewed and uncrewed Mercury flights. By the time John Glenn flew, Kranz was the assistant flight director.
"Mercury was our training ground, our bootcamp for what space was all about," Kranz said.

Kranz was named flight director during the Gemini program, and work then started on the Apollo program. Unfortunately, the Apollo 1 mission never got off the ground. Kranz had worked doing a "plugs in test," during which power wasn't transferred to the space vessel, the day before the fatal fire. There had been problems with communications and life support, as well as deviations throughout the test.

The day of the fire, Kranz had been doing early testing prep work for the "plugs out test," where there would be power. He handed the test over at noon and went home at about 3 p.m. to take his wife out, after the birth of their third child. As they were getting ready, he got a knock on the door telling him there had been an accident and the crew of Apollo 1 had died. The area around Mission Control was locked down and Kranz had to use a freight entrance to get into the operations room.

"I basically witnessed firsthand the impact upon the young people on the Mission Control team," Kranz said, adding he had lost people in Korea and knew about losses. Some of those under him in Mission Control had never known loss like that before that day.

"It was a question of carrying this young group of people through a very traumatic event," he remarked. "It was traumatic in many ways. We not only lost a crew, but there was a good chance the program was under a great threat. ... We now had to mature a tough and competent flight control team. ... I addressed the people three days after. I'm assuming the responsibility for our part of the failure. We didn't bother searching for who was responsible. We just assumed we were responsible."

Kranz talk became known as the Kranz Dictum, "tough and competent" speech — a phrase that was written on a blackboard and would not be erased until a man landed on the moon.

"I concluded the talk identifying the problem throughout all of our preparation for Apollo 1 was the fact that we were not tough enough," Kranz confirmed. "We were avoiding our responsibilities. We had not assumed the accountability we should have for what was going on during that day's test. We had the opportunity to call it all off, to say 'this isn't right. Let's shut it down,' and none of us did. So basically the toughness was from that day forward we would stand for doing everything right, literally being perfect and competent."

Several changes were made afterward not only on the vessel, but in management as well. Kranz became a division chief of flight directors for Apollo. He worked as a flight director only on odd numbered Apollo missions — that meant he was director for Apollo 11, the first lunar landing, and Apollo 13. While Apollo 11 set history with the first lunar landing and was deemed a success, Kranz remembers everything that went wrong that day.

"We had massive communications problems ... The second thing was basically a procedure issue related to the separation between the two spacecraft. The crew didn't fully vent the pressure in the tunnel between the two spacecraft and when they separated it was like a champagne cork popping out of a bottle. So this is going to change our trajectory, it's going to change the point where we start the descent to the surface of the moon. The third one was that the computer started to have a series of fault downs," he stated.

Kranz had to decide, based on the communications issues, whether to continue the descent to the moon.

"I made the go/no go to go down to the surface of the moon based on the gut feeling that my team would solve the problem and we would continue down for five minutes and if we didn't then we would have to abort the landing," Kranz said.

With the trajectory changed, more fuel was used than originally planned. Mission Control officials did a countdown of the seconds of fuel left as Neil Armstrong looked to land on the lunar surface. Kranz praised Armstrong as "the perfect pilot" enabling him to pilot down to the moon with the computer faults.

Then they heard "Houston, Tranquility Base here. The Eagle has landed."

While the viewing room and world erupted into applause, Kranz and officials still had a lot of work to do.

"I just wish we could do it one more time and this time celebrate with the world," he observed.

Kranz next was the flight director for Apollo 13 — the lunar flight that never got to the moon.
The first indication something was wrong was an alert, which at the time was believed to be an "instrumentation problem," when the vessel was in orbit. It was something much worse. An explosion in oxygen tank 2 damaged the spacecraft, making it unable to complete its mission and putting the lives of astronauts Jim Lovell, Jack Swigert, and Fred Haise in jeopardy.

"It became a mission of survival," Kranz confirmed, adding the challenge was how to make a two-day spacecraft into a lifeboat and find a way home.

Kranz and his team handed off the responsibility of running Mission Control, and got to work solving all the problems Apollo 13 would have getting home. Later, when asked if anyone was panicked about the issues with Apollo 13, Kranz firmly stated no.

"When bad things happen, we just calmly lay out all the options, and failure was not one of them," he stated.

The paraphrase of "failure is not an option," would follow Kranz throughout his life.

"We had to invent all kinds of workarounds to address every problem that we saw," Kranz recalled. "Basically our belief, my belief, our belief as a team, [was] always give us any problem and that's when we operate best. We're problem solvers so give us something that's tough. That's the mood we carried to the end of the mission."

The hard work of Kranz and his team prevailed, and Apollo 13 splashed down April 17, 1970. Images at the time show Kranz and other flight directors cheering from Mission Control as the three astronauts returned to Earth. When asked if that was his greatest moment in Mission Control, Kranz replied that there were a lot of great moments.

"The greatest moment was always the satisfaction at the end of the mission of my team's performance," he stated.

Kranz continued to work for NASA, being promoted to deputy director of mission operations in 1974 and director in 1983. He was in Mission Control when the Space Shuttle Challenger was lost in 1986. He retired from NASA in 1994.

Despite being retired, Kranz has kept extremely busy. He has earned countless honors for this work, including the Presidential Medal of Freedom, two NASA Exceptional Service Medals, and NASA Outstanding Leadership Medals. He has been inducted into the National Aviation Hall of Fame, has had the Toledo Express Airport and schools named after him, and was awarded the Michael Collins Trophy for Lifetime Achievement from the Smithsonian National Air and Space Museum.

In 1995, the movie "Apollo 13" came out. There now was a motion picture that highlighted some of the key things Kranz and his team did to help save the Apollo 13 astronauts. In 2000, his autobiography, Failure Is Not an Option, was published. It was later adapted into a documentary. He released another book in 2023, entitled Tough and Competent: Leadership and Team Chemistry. The book talks about how NASA's Mission Control teams worked together to create a dynasty capable of problem-solving and more.

Kranz also had a passion project. In 2017, he directed the restoration of the Mission Control Room at the Johnson Space Center so it looked how it did during the Apollo program. He also continues to advocate for the U.S. space program. In 2011, he spoke to the Senate Aviation and Space Subcommittee about the future of space exploration. He stressed the need for the United States to continue exploring space.

"Our aerospace industry is the envy of the world, employing 650,000 Americans in high-wage, high-skill jobs," he testified. "It is one of our few industries that actually enjoys a trade surplus with our foreign competition. Every time NASA accomplishes a great achievement, the interest of our young people in pursuing a career in science and engineering spikes upward. When those kids graduate from college, they may not all end up working in the space program, but many of them end up with leading commercial technology businesses in Silicon Valley and elsewhere."

Kranz however lamented the gap between the space shuttle program and the next manned space projects in the United States, calling it an "impractical, shortsighted approach." He urged Congress and the nation to use its necessary resources to invest in the future of the nation's space exploration.

"We need to limit the duration of the U.S. human space flight gap and prevent it from growing, to forestall the hemorrhaging of our talented and experienced aerospace workforce and supplier network," he stated.

Today, Kranz continues to advocate for the future of U.S. space exploration while keeping an eye on the projects NASA has underway.

A Legacy Larger than Life: Commemorating the enduring impact of an astronaut's journey and the collective memory of what pushes humanity further.

Charles Bassett II

*"For a boy who watched planes soar, Charles Bassett II
turned dreams into flight, blending the wisdom of a scientist with
the courage of an explorer. His journey from Ohio's skies to reaching for
space's vast frontiers reminds us that the path to the stars
is paved with dedication, education, and the unyielding
pursuit of one's passion."*

Charles Arthur "Art" Bassett II always loved the idea of flight, and he wasn't afraid to work toward his goal of soaring in the heavens. Bassett was born in Dayton, Ohio. His father was an Air Force colonel, and as a youth Bassett would watch airplanes take off. Soon, he became enamored with flight.

"I guess I was one of the few lucky people who knew right from the day he was born what he wanted to do and then was able to do it," Bassett once remarked.

He took part in a model plane club while in high school in Berea, building gasoline-powered models, which he flew in the school's gym. Wanting to learn to fly actual airplanes, Bassett earned money for lessons by greasing and fueling planes at an airport near Cleveland. He took his first solo flight as a pilot when he was 16. At 17, he had his private flying license. Learning to fly was just the beginning of Bassett's love for aviation. He also wanted to learn more.

He attended Ohio State University from 1950-52, studying aeronautical engineering. He left in 1952, enrolling in the U.S. Air Force as an aviation cadet. A little more than a year later, he earned a commission in the Air Force. He became an Air Force pilot in Korea and would later earn the Air Force Commendation Ribbon for bravery.

Bassett worked hard to graduate from Aerospace Research Pilot School and then the Air Force Experimental Pilot School. He served as an experimental test pilot as well as an engineering test pilot at Edwards Air Force Base. He worked his way up to captain by January 1960. Striving to learn more, Bassett attended Texas Technological College from 1958-60, where he earned a Bachelor of Science degree in electrical engineering. He completed some graduate work at the University of Southern California.

In 1961, NASA announced the Apollo Space Program with the goal of sending a man to the moon. Bassett put in his application. In 1963, NASA announced that more than 700 applications had been received to be part of the third group of astronauts in that program. Only 14 were selected, and Bassett was among them. During the NASA Group 3 press conference in 1963, Bassett was asked how important a science degree was to an astronaut.

"I think it would be pretty important just because it would give them an understanding of what he's doing and why," he responded. "You have to know how to talk to people, particularly the learned engineers and scientists that he will be discussing problems with. I think it's important to have a common bond of understanding."

During his career with NASA, Bassett acted as a ground communicator for Gemini 7 in December 1965. He also would have responsibilities relating to training and simulations. Bassett told individuals during a trip to the Lewis Research Center that he had studied "about every phase of space science there is."

"It's my job now to keep current on the constantly changing technical information and keep doing the best I can on everything," he elaborated.

While acting as ground communicator for Gemini 7, Bassett was the one to tell astronauts Jim Lovell and Frank Borman they would be able to land before the start of their 207th orbit.

"The blue team is happy to give you a go for the big 207-1 (landing)," he stated, later mentioning that they were flying on the 62nd anniversary of the Wright brothers' first airplane flight.

Though he was serious in his training, Bassett still found ways to have fun. One example is during a weightless flight test over Dayton in 1964, he acted like Superman when he pushed off from the side of the cabin.

"I'm lucky to be in the space program and wouldn't trade it for anything," Bassett said.

Though busy with his duties as an astronaut, Bassett took time to talk to school children about space, as well as the need for education. He even penned an article highlighting the need for space exploration, after some members of the public questioned the benefits versus the cost of the space program.

In 1965, Bassett wrote an article in the Tuscarama Home & Community talking about why America should go to the moon.

"...to the astronauts, engineers and scientists, indeed to all the tens of thousands of personnel all over our country involved in this vast project, the earnest preparations are charged with a rare sense of dedication and with a powerful unity of purpose," he wrote. "It is sometimes surprising to me as an astronaut to realize that many people still feel that placing man on the moon and returning him to earth is our only objective in space."

Bassett stressed that exploring the moon "is only man's first stepping stone into space." Bassett felt that America was not content to sit back and watch other countries explore space.

"It is far more in keeping with our heritage that we deliberately set a difficult national goal [to get to the moon] than merely respond to the accomplishments of other nations," he reflected. Bassett also stressed that the nation's youth were excited about the prospect of space travel.

"The character traits necessary to partake in this adventure are traits that we would like to see developed in our youngsters — intelligence, integrity, objectivity, common sense, and a host of others," he expressed.

Going to the moon would benefit not only the United States, but the world in general. He felt that going to the moon could reveal secrets of the formation of Earth and the solar system.

"Other benefits — perhaps the greatest of all — are in the progress of the unforeseen," Bassett hypothesized. "Progress cannot be visualized in advance."

When asked about his chances of going to the moon during a talk in 1964, Bassett said he hoped they were good, but knew he was competing with "some of the most competent people in the world."

Though it wasn't a moon shot yet, Bassett must have been excited in November 1965 when it was announced that he would be the copilot of Gemini 9 and would be the second American to walk in space during the flight. NASA planned for him to be outside the capsule for about an hour and a half. Bassett along with Elliott See Jr. would crew the Gemini 9. The two men were asked for the 1966 World Book encyclopedia to write statements about their upcoming mission.

"I haven't done much with my life yet, but someday I'll orbit the Earth," he quipped. A man who believed strongly in education, he wrote,"It's worth 33 years of school to get a chance to go to the moon."

Unfortunately, Bassett and See would never see their Gemini flight. On Feb. 28, 1966, the two were flying in a T-38 military training jet to St. Louis for simulator training on the Gemini spacecraft when something went wrong. See radioed astronauts Thomas Stafford and Eugene Cernan, who were following them, that he had to do a vision landing at the airport as it was covered in fog and rain. The T-38's wing would clip the roof of the building that held the Gemini 9, causing the T-38's fuselage to go across the roof before hitting the ground in an explosion. Neither man survived.

"Both of these men were fine persons and excellent professional test pilots," said Robert Gilruth, director of the Manned Spacecraft Center. "We will miss them more than I can say."

Bassett is buried in Arlington National Cemetery. While Bassett never saw his dream of reaching the moon become reality, his fellow astronauts found a way to honor his drive to the moon. The crew of Apollo 15 placed a small sculpture on the moon in 1971 honoring the astronauts who lost their lives reaching for the stars — Bassett's name is the first on the sculpture.

"We just thought we'd recognize the guys that made the ultimate contribution," said astronaut David Scott.

Bassett's name also appears on the Kennedy Space Center's Space Mirror Memorial. Bassett's daughter, Karen Stevenson, has spoken at NASA's Day of Remembrance ceremony at the Kennedy Space Center, in his honor as well. Bassett is among those remembered each year at the ceremony.

"The legacy of those who have perished is present every day in our work and inspires generations of new space explorers," NASA administrator Charles Bolden said in a statement during the ceremony. "Every day, with each new challenge we overcome and every discovery we make, we honor these remarkable men and women."

In 2019, a mural featuring Bassett was unveiled in downtown Dayton, thanks to donations from the public and funds from the National Aviation Heritage Area. Over the years, his alma mater also has worked to honor Bassett. In 1993, he was honored with a distinguished engineer citation. In 1996, Texas Tech University dedicated its electrical engineering research laboratory in Bassett's honor.

"This is a fitting tribute to a man who dedicated his life to pursuing the dream of space flight," said Daniel Goldin, who was NASA's administrator during the lab's dedication ceremony. "It is gratifying to know that the laboratory bearing his name will help to encourage today's students to achieve their own personal goals."

"This is a tremendous honor and a generous remembrance of Charlie's life and accomplishments," said George W. S. Abbey, director of the Johnson Space Center where Bassett trained. "We share the pride that Charlie's family feels with this dedication of the Charles A. Bassett Laboratories. This dedication reflects Charlie's own strong beliefs in the value of education and perseverance."

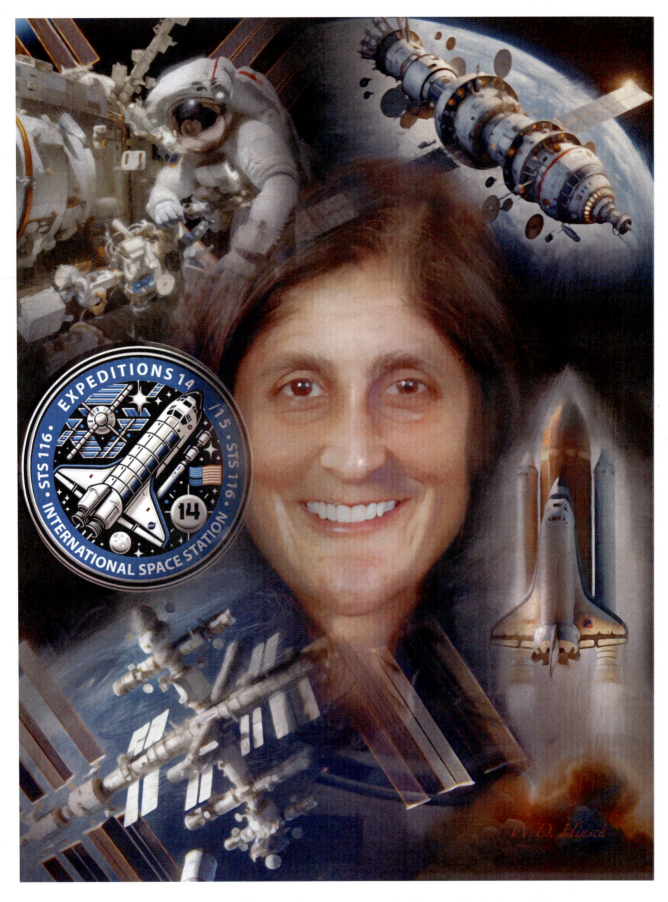

Eyes on the Horizon: Reflecting the aspirations of all humankind, she celebrates the pioneering spirit that propels us toward the stars

Sunita Williams

"Dream big, work hard, stay humble, and surround yourself with positive people," Sunita Williams often said, a mantra she not only preaches but lives by.

Sometimes life leads you down an unexpected path and suddenly, you find yourself walking among the stars. For Sunita Williams, that certainly was the case.

Williams was born Sept. 19, 1965, in Euclid. When she was young, her parents moved the family to Needham, Mass., where she graduated high school in 1983. Growing up, Williams wanted to be a veterinarian. She wanted to study veterinary sciences at Harvard but didn't get admitted. She received a scholarship from Columbia but didn't like New York. Her brother suggested the naval academy.

Williams enrolled in the U.S. Navy Academy, where she earned her Bachelor of Science in physical science in 1987 then received her commission as an ensign in the U.S. Navy. She spent six months at Naval Coastal System Command before receiving a designation as a basic diving officer, reporting to Naval Aviation Training Command. In 1989, she became a naval aviator and completed helicopter combat support training. Willams decided to pursue flying over diving for the Navy.

"I was thinking the better, more fun life will be flying," she stated during an interview with Cape Cod Wave Magazine. "Everything is romanticized by jets. Of course, that's what I wanted to do. Don't forget how old I was. I was 21, 22 at the time. That was sort of the thing to do. But I didn't get jets. I was a helicopter pilot."

She later would be deployed to help support Operation Desert Shield and Operation Provide Comfort in the Mediterranean, Red Sea, and Persian Gulf area. After Hurricane Andrew struck the United States, she was named the officer in charge of a detachment sent to Miami, Fla., to help with relief operations.

In 1993, Williams was selected for the U.S. Naval Test Pilot School. Upon graduation, she was assigned various tasks including a squadron safety officer, chase pilot, and project officer. She flew test flights in several aircraft in those positions. In 1995, she returned to Naval Test Pilot School as an instructor in the Rotary Wing Department and was the school's safety officer. As part of test pilot school, Williams came to Johnson Space Center to see all the simulators. It was then she realized there were other helicopter pilots who were astronauts.

"So I started looking up the application," she stated.

Her first application was rejected. She was told she needed more education. She then attended Florida Institute of Technology, earning a Master of Science degree in engineering management in 1995. A few years later, she decided to reapply to NASA. By that time, Williams was assigned to the USS Saipan as the aircraft handler and assistant air boss. She was deployed on the USS Saipan when she learned she had been selected for the astronaut program.

"I was living on the ship and everyone had left when the phone rang," she recalled, stating the caller asked her, 'Are you interested in coming to Johnson Space Center to work in the astronaut program?' "

Williams was accepted as an astronaut in 1998, though it would be eight years before her first flight. She would serve as a liaison in Moscow to support Expedition 1 and station robotics work for the ISS. In 2002, she was asked if she wanted to go to the ISS. The answer was yes.

One of the first things Williams did was take part in the NASA Extreme Environment Mission Operations (NEEMO) as part of her training. She was part of the second group of NEEMO, which sends astronauts, engineers, and scientists to live in an underwater laboratory off of Key Largo, Fla. There, crew members prepare for future space missions including performing EVAs in an underwater environment. Williams was there for seven days from May 13-20, 2002. She had other training as well, but then tragedy struck when the Columbia Space Shuttle disintegrated upon re-entry to Earth in 2003.

"The overwhelming emotion was disbelief," Williams said. "Secondly, we just lost seven friends."

All space shuttle flights were suspended for several years while NASA officials worked to find the cause and make adjustments to the remaining shuttles to prevent another tragedy.

"Those people went to space knowing the dangers," she said, speaking at the Space & Science Festival in New York. "We want to continue their legacy and make what they did worthwhile."

Williams became part of Expedition 14 on the ISS. Expedition 14 continued the assembly of the ISS, including reconfiguring the power from the solar arrays and cooling system, removing shrouds from the truss system, and other tasks. The Space Shuttle Discovery would drop Williams off on the ISS. There, she would act as the station's flight engineer. Discovery also would carry the P5 Truss segment of the ISS. The shuttle launched Dec. 9, 2006, and docked Dec. 11 at the ISS.

While Discovery was still docked, Williams conducted her first Spacewalk on ISS — helping rewire the station, install a robotic arm grapple fixture, and position debris shield panels.

"Honestly I was not scared at first," she admitted of her first spacewalk on Dec. 15, 2006. "It was nighttime. Everything is very well choreographed and planned. I knew exactly what I was doing. And then the sun came up."

The sun then came up. Light struck the planet and shuttle, and Williams took a moment to look in awe.

"Holy crap. We are flying across the planet and I am sitting here outside in my suit," she said was her first thought.

On Dec. 19, 2006, Discovery separated from the ISS, taking Thomas Reiter of the European Space Agency back to Earth.

"When you see that shuttle leave and fly away, your stomach drops," Williams admitted, adding the thought "Oh crap, they're going to Earth. I'm here" popped into her head. In a way, it was like being on Navy deployment. Williams kept busy on the ISS, especially with her spacewalks.

"Maybe I have low expectations, but I never had an idea of how cool it was going to be to really live in space and adapt to space and just feel like you're at home in space," Williams told the Johnson Space Center Oral History Project. "That's what Expedition 14 did for me, and part of that was three spacewalks with L.A. (Michael Lopez-Alegria)."

During her time with Expedition 14, Williams set a new world record for the most spacewalks for a woman with her four spacewalks, which totaled 29 hours and 17 minutes. The record was broken in 2008 by astronaut Peggy Whitson. In addition to setting the world record, Williams also took part in a first for mankind. On April 16, 2007, Williams became the first person to run a marathon in space. She was listed as a runner in the Boston Marathon. She took part in the marathon the following year as well.

Williams' first trip to the ISS was to last only six months. However, poor weather caused her flight home to be delayed. She was in space 195 days. It was the record for the longest single spaceflight by a woman — a record she held until 2015 when Samantha Cristoforetti broke it. Williams returned to Earth on June 22, 2007, onboard the Space Shuttle Atlantis. While she was happy to be back, after experiencing weightlessness for six months, gravity "hit [her] like a ton of bricks."

"Little things like lifting up your head with your neck takes work," she admitted. "Your head feels heavy. The muscles [in your neck] haven't had anything to do for six months. Eventually you get it back again. Initially, it's tough."

Upon her return to Earth, Williams served as deputy chief of the astronaut office. Williams returned to the ISS again in 2002 as part of Expedition 32/33. She served as flight engineer for Expedition 32. On July 15, 2012, Williams, along with cosmonaut Yuri Malenchenko and Akihiko Hoshide of the Japan Aerospace Exploration Agency, took off from the Baikonur Cosmodrone in Kazakhstan onboard a Russian spacecraft. Their destination was the ISS.

The three were welcomed onto the ISS on July 17, 2012. Williams spent the next four months conducting research and making repairs. The crew conducted Earth observations, experiments on how microgravity affects spinal cords, software tests to alter communication radios, monitor immune functions, and more. Williams became commander of the ISS on Sept. 17, 2012, as part of the Expedition 33 team. The same month, Williams marked another first for the space program, becoming the first person to take part in a triathlon in space as part of the Nautica Malibu Triathlon.

While she couldn't do the swimming portion, she used the station's advanced resistive exercise device to do weightlifting and resistance exercises to approximate swimming. While she was on the ISS in 2012, she also ran a blog called "Space to Run" to keep people informed of what was happening on the space station.

"I think one of the coolest things about being on a long-duration space mission is you can gather people who have like interests with you and tell them about what you're doing in space," she said during an interview for the Johnson Space Center Oral History Project. "It's hard when you just see somebody one time to really get them excited about space, unless they go see a launch, or something like that, or watch a spacewalk. It's like, 'Oh wow!' Or they have a direct connection with you. I think the blog was pretty neat, because I tried to talk about things that people on the ground are familiar with. What cool parts of the Earth did we fly over? Every week I did a blog."

She wrote about food in space, things she saw out the window, workouts, experiments, and the geography she could see on Earth.

"It was consistent, to try to keep people tied in to what's going on in space," she said. "I think one of the cool things about that [is] that went to a lot of different teachers. I was in touch with my sixth-grade teacher, Angela DiNapoli, and everybody in Needham, Mass., got those blogs. All my cousins who have kids who are going to school [have] got all those blogs. Kids got to read it every week, so that's cool. ...You can drag all those people into space life, because they're living it with you."

Williams had a lot of interesting stories to tell, especially about her spacewalks. During one spacewalk, Williams and Hoshide used a toothbrush to help install a replacement main-bus switch unit, which was one of four boxes responsible for routing power from the solar panels to the ISS. One of the two bolts to secure the unit got stuck as there was debris inside the bolt receptacle. The brush was used to clear the debris and help lubricate the threats of the bolt.

Williams along with Hoshide and Malenchenko returned to Earth on Nov 19, 2012. Thus far in her career as an astronaut, Williams has spent 322 days in space. Williams retired from the U.S. Navy with the rank of captain in May 2017. She remains in the astronaut program.

In 2017, Needham, Mass., announced they were naming an elementary school after her. Williams even has a day named after her, celebrated at the elementary school. The first Sunita Williams Day was held there on May 22, 2023. Williams spent the day going to various classes to talk to students and spoke during a school assembly.

"I'm very honored the school is named after me. I recognize I have a very unique job and when I was in these guys' [the students'] shoes, I didn't really have that idea I would even be able to be an astronaut," Williams said, adding that she enjoyed talking to the students not only about what she's accomplished but what NASA is doing and the plans for the future.

The honor is just one of many Williams has earned. She has been awarded a Navy Commendation Medal, Navy and Marine Achievement Medal, Service Medal, and NASA Spaceflight Medal. Internationally, she has been awarded the Russian Medal for Merit in Space Exploration, Padma Bhushan Civilian Award from India, and the Sardar Vallabhbhai Patel Vishwa Pratibha Award.

Williams is currently training to take part in Boeing's Starliner spacecraft crewed mission in 2024. Williams and astronaut Butch Wilmore are scheduled to fly Starliner to the ISS and remain docked there for several weeks to evaluate the spacecraft and its systems.

Dreams of the Cosmos: His example of ambition and the enduring human quest for discovery, symbolized by his awe-inspiring journey into space, started with the wanderlust of a kid from the heartland.

Terence 'Tom' Henricks

"From rural roots to cosmic heights — Tom Henricks' story is a tale of perseverance and breaking barriers marked him as a leader in life, and space."

Don't ever sell your dreams short. You never know how far they may be able to soar; just ask astronaut Terence "Tom" Henricks. Henricks was born July 5, 1952, in Bryan, Ohio. While he was born in Bryan, Henricks considered Woodville, Ohio, where he graduated high school in 1970, more of his hometown.

Henricks first became interested in flight when he was 12 and his grandparents gave him money for a plane ride at the Woodruff Airport in Montpelier. It was a love of aviation that would eventually lead him to fly more than 30 different types of aircraft. He never dreamed a space vessel would be one of them.

Henricks grew up on a farm and no one in his family had gone to college before him. He recalled going through school during the Mercury, Gemini, and Apollo space programs. He kept a scrapbook of those missions and loved the idea of space exploration. He just didn't think he would ever see space.

In a 2019 interview by the News-Messenger, Henricks said even though he stayed up late to watch the moon landing on TV when he was 17, the idea of being an astronaut never really crossed his mind.

"At the time, I didn't consider being an astronaut, even though we [Ohioans] had Neil Armstrong and John Glenn," he reflected. "I just didn't think that someone from a small town could be chosen."

Henricks now realizes he was selling his dreams short. It's something he warns students and others against when he speaks to crowds today.

"The way I explain it to young people now is not to set their goals short, they can dream big. When I was on the farm, I just wanted to get through college. Then, at the Air Force Academy, I could be a pilot. I never considered being an astronaut until I was older. So I was selling myself short for no reason. So I try to encourage young people not to set artificial barriers to their dreams," he stated during an interview for Arabic Knowledge at Wharton.

Before he could see the stars, Henricks needed an education. Henricks received his Bachelor of Science in civil engineering from the U.S. Air Force Academy in 1974. He then completed pilot training at Craig Air Force Base and F-4 conversion training. Henricks went on to receive his Master of Public Administration from Golden State University in 1982. Henricks then attended the U.S. Air Forces' Test Pilot School in 1983 becoming a F-16C test pilot and chief of the 57th Fighter Weapons Wing Operating Location. He earned the Distinguished Flying Cross, Air Force Meritorious Service Medal and two Air Force Commendation Medals. He also received the F-4 Fight Weapons School Outstanding Flying Award.

In 1976, the Air Force and NASA started to recruit pilots to be astronauts in order to fly the space shuttles.

"Even though I was still a young lieutenant I applied because I thought 'well now they're asking guys like me to go into space. Maybe I have a chance,'" he recalled. He applied four times to the program before he was accepted. "Persistence was key for that."

The fourth time he applied, Henricks was a bit nervous. NASA had an age limitation on applicants for Air Force pilots. He was nearing that age. Henricks didn't need to worry. NASA selected Henricks in 1985 for the program.

"I was just stunned," he recalled during an interview with Airplane Academy. "It changed my life."

Henricks would have several technical assignments outside of going to space for NASA. He helped re-evaluate shuttle landing sites across the globe and acted as assistant manager for engineering integration in the space program office. He was lead astronaut of the Shuttle Avionics Integration Laboratory and of the Vehicle Test and Checkout. He also was chief of the Astronaut Office Operations Development Branch and assistant for the shuttle to the chief of the astronaut office. During a United Press International interview in November 1991, Henricks expressed his excitement as he looked forward to his first space mission.

"I want to feel the sensation of the solid rocket motors igniting. I want to feel that sensation when the main engines cut off and you float in your seat. I want to remember that mental image of the Earth view the first time we see it," Henricks said. "The apprehension or anxiety I feel, when I have the time to sit back and think about it, is not fear of physical harm, it's fear of not doing my best," he added.

Henricks first saw space onboard the Space Shuttle Atlantis in 1991. He served as pilot for the mission. Despite Henricks' first flight being years after the Challenger disaster, some people were still nervous about liftoffs. The father of three had to deal with anxiety from not just the public, but his children.

"The second and third grader are old enough to know what's going on and they get questions about, can the shuttle explode, and of course, I have to answer yes, it could," Henricks admitted during a 1991 interview. "But it's as safe as we can make it and I'm prepared and that's my job and even if something happens they're taken care of and they're loved. So I don't try to avoid the issue with them. They're looking forward to going down to (the) launch."

The launch was delayed a few times. It was initially set for Nov. 19, 1991, but was delayed due to a malfunction on a unit for the upper state booster. A date of Nov. 24 was set then. There was a slight delay of thirteen minutes at that time to allow an orbiting spacecraft to pass over the launch site as well as to replenish external liquid oxygen tanks. The shuttle then launched at night on Nov. 24, 1991.

Its primary mission was to deploy a Defense Support Program satellite.
In addition to the satellite, the crew carried with it several monitors and experiments including the Air Force Maui Optical System, a cosmic radiation effects and activation monitor, an extended duration orbiter medical project, and a bioreactor flow and particle trajectory experiment. The crew also used a telescope, cameras, and binoculars to observe U.S. military installations from space, because Pentagon officials wanted to know how much detail could be picked up from orbit.

Shuttle crews also had some fun as they were woken on Nov. 25, 1991, by a recorded call by Patrick Stewart, who played Captain Jean-Luc Picard on Star Trek: The Next Generation.
"Space: the final frontier," Stewart quipped. "This is the voyage of the Space Shuttle Atlantis. Its ten-day mission: To explore new methods of remote sensing and observation of the planet Earth ... To seek out new data on radiation in space, and a new understanding of the effects of microgravity on the human body ... To boldly go where 255 men and women have gone before."

Atlantis touched down on Dec. 8, 1991, as a success. Henrick's second flight was two years later onboard the Space Shuttle Columbia. He would once again serve as the pilot. This time the launch was delayed several times for a variety of reasons including to replace all three turbopumps, hydraulic line issues, incomplete ignition (the third in NASA's history) and faulty readings. The shuttle finally launched on April 26, 1993.

The mission, which included the second German Spacelab, had 33 experiments ranging from material and life sciences to technology applications and astronomy/atmospheric physics. The shuttle had an advanced mini-diagnostic laboratory for the "most comprehensive medical screening to date of human adaptation to weightlessness." Crews also continued the SAREX radio program and communicated with children around the world about what was happening during the mission.

Unfortunately, there were several problems onboard the flight. An overheating refrigerator/freezer forced crews to backup stored experiment samples. There was a leak in the nitrogen line in the shuttle's wastewater tank. An "errant command" from Mission Control also caused communications to be lost with Columbia for more than an hour several days into their mission.

The shuttle would land on May 6, 1993, after nearly ten days in space. Back on Earth, Henricks was honored with an honorary Doctor of Science degree in 1993 from Defiance College. His next flight was two years later in 1995. Nicknamed the "All-Ohio" crew, the entire crew was made up of Ohioans except for Kevin Kregel of New York. He was made an honorary Ohio citizen by Gov. George Voinovich just prior to the launch on July 13, 1995. Henricks was commander of the mission.

The Space Shuttle Discovery's mission was to launch the seventh tracking and data relay satellite as well as conduct several experiments. With an "all-Ohio" crew, most people would think a Buckeye would be the mission's unofficial mascot, but instead it was a woodpecker. The reason for this unlikely mascot was that a woodpecker had delayed the launch of the shuttle for a month after it drilled hundreds of holes into the foam insulation surrounding the shuttle's external tank. The shuttle had to be taken off the pad for repairs.

One of the wake-up calls for the Ohio crew poked fun at the situation: the theme song from "Woody Woodpecker." During the week, the calls had a more 'Ohio' theme, with "Beautiful Ohio" as well as the Cleveland Indians baseball song.

In orbit, the crew worked hard on launching the satellite and on various experiments. Henricks worked with a video camera that had been designed to pinpoint the latitude and longitude of areas that were being videotaped. While researchers were happy with the photos, the crew wasn't. They had a lot of trouble focusing the camera.

"We tried every trick we could think of," Henricks would tell Mission Control.

The crew also was part of a dedication ceremony for the new integrated consolidated control center. While a ceremony was taking place on Earth, the crew videoed in for an in-orbit dedication ceremony.

"We'd like to share a moment with you to dedicate the new consolidated control center," Henricks stated from orbit. "After 30 years of hard work which included over 100 manned space flights from our old control room, we're now entering the next century by opening the new control center which will lead our manned spaceflight program into future benefits aboard the International Space Station and into the next century continuing our exploration of the solar system for the benefit of humankind."

Discovery touched down on July 22, 1995, ending the all-Ohio mission.

Henrick's fourth flight was onboard the Space Shuttle Columbia. He was the mission commander once more. Launched on June 20, 1996, the mission would become the longest to date at sixteen days. The flight would be the first to have an in-cabin camera to provide video images from the flight deck. It would include microgravity studies and life science investigations that would serve as a model for studies on board the International Space Station. The Life and Microgravity Spacelab was a collaboration between scientists from ten counties as well as five space agencies. Examples of the experiments included: bone and muscle loss in space, a comprehensive study of sleep cycles in microgravity, solidifying zirconia particles, and more.

It was during his fourth mission Henricks decided it was time to retire. His last mission had made him the first person to log more than 1,000 hours as a space shuttle pilot/commander. He had earned the NASA Outstanding Leadership Medal, Defense Superior Service Medal, Defense Meritorious Service Medal, and four NASA Space Flight Medals.

"We had a quiet moment, and I decided, looking down at the Earth, that I'd had my fair share of space flight, and I didn't have to risk my life to experience it again," he stated. "I had satisfied my personal goals as an astronaut."

His children — who were 14, 12 and 8 at the time — convinced him it was the right decision. Henricks retired from NASA in 1997. He worked on the corporate management team of Timken Aerospace, then as an executive with Textron. He went on to be president of McGraw-Hill's Aviation Week. He then joined Corporate Aviation Analysis & Planning, where he serves as a consultant and vice president of marketing. Henricks told The Plain Dealer in 2008 that he had to work to prove himself outside of being an astronaut after leaving NASA.

"Some name recognition can be a hindrance once you leave NASA," he explained. "A number of us are now in other careers, and in my own personal experience, I had to distance myself a bit from relying on just being an astronaut. When you go out in the marketplace you still have to prove yourself in the new world. And if you're a celebrity I think that's more challenging."

Henricks continues to be an active pilot.

"I want to take my grandchildren flying," he said of his future goals. "I've taken my children flying. I want to get my grandchildren interested in aviation and space." Henricks said the future is happening now in space with private flights on vessels such as SpaceX and the Starliner.

"It is opening up the opportunity for almost everyone to go to space," he exclaimed. "You won't have to be a test pilot. You won't have to be a government employee. You won't even have to be rich. The price is going to drop.

"The diversity of needs in space is already expanding.... We have a space station that has been up for two decades. We need people to maintain that. As we go further out into space, back to the moon and onto Mars we need plumbers, construction workers — a diverse group of needs. Artists! Just as aviation expanded during the first half of the 19th century, travel in space will expand in the first half of this century."

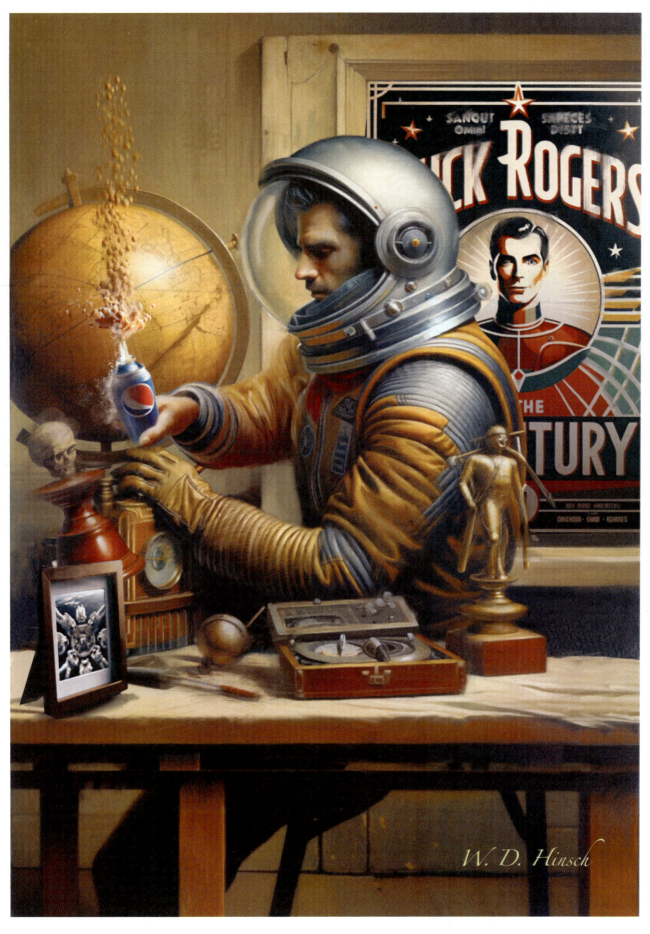

Contemplating the Cosmos: The introspective moments of an astronaut, contemplating the mysteries of space over a can of cosmic cola.

Dr. Karl Henize

"Like Buck Rogers, a childhood hero, Dr. Karl Henize turned his starry-eyed dreams into a stellar reality. From the starry skies over Ohio to the luminous vastness of space, his journey exemplifies the spirit of adventure, proving that the universe is not just a playground of the imagination, but a frontier awaiting the footsteps of the daring and the curious."

Two things can be said for certain about Dr. Karl Henize — he loved the stars and a challenge. The Cincinnati native was a renowned astronomer before he joined the space program. His interest in space began as a child with a love of Buck Rogers, and the heavenly skies seen from his home along a hilly pasture near Plainsville, Ohio.

"We were a quarter of a mile from the next closest neighbor, so we had really dark skies," Henize said in a 1985 interview with the Cincinnati Enquirer. "The stars just jump out at you. It was hard not to get excited about them."

He loved Buck Rogers, but he knew that the science fiction serial about a man who travels the stars was pure fantasy. Any U.S. space program in Henize's youth in the 1930s was fiction as well. Despite space travel being nothing but a fantasy at the time, Henize wouldn't give up on the stars.

"I thought that if I couldn't go out there myself, I at least wanted to look at these things," he reflected in the Enquirer interview. Henize did a lot more than look.

He began his career as an astrophysicist in 1948 at the University of Michigan Observatory. It was there he began his survey of the southern sky, looking for stars and nebulae that showed hydrogen emission lines. In 1954, he became a fellow at the Mount Wilson Observatory in Pasadena, California, where he continued to study those emission-line stars and nebulae.

In 1956, he began his tenure as the senior astronomer at the Smithsonian Astrophysical Observatory, according to NASA. His job there was to handle photographic satellite tracking stations for the satellite tracking program. He also was responsible for establishing and operating a global network of twelve stations for photographic tracking of artificial Earth satellites.

In 1956, Henize also released the results of an extensive survey he had done looking at the dwarf galaxy (also known as a Magellanic Cloud or irregular galaxy) nearest to Earth, which is only visible in the southern hemisphere. Parts of that galaxy are referred to as the Large Magellanic Cloud (LMC) and Small Magellanic Cloud (SMC). Henize examined both and cataloged all the interesting objects, such as emission-line stars and nebulae, he found. These "interesting objects" now bear his name and are being examined more closely.

According to NASA, during Henize's life he discovered more than 2,000 stars in the southern hemisphere, designated as "HE" in star catalogs. One example is the dwarf starburst galaxy classified as Henize 2-10. According to a press release from the Hubble Space Telescope in 2022, a black hole there is not "tearing apart stars, consuming anything that comes too close" but instead is doing the opposite as there is "a gas outflow stretching from the black hole to a bright star birth region like an umbilical cord."

Henize continued his work in astronomy, becoming an associate then professor of astronomy at Northwestern University. When the United States began its Mercury Space Program in the late 1950s, Henize's interest in space travel blazed even more brightly. He designed a small hand-held camera for use by Gemini astronauts. He also became the principal investigator of an experiment to obtain ultraviolet stellar spectra during the Gemini 10, 11 and 12 flights, according to the book NASA's Scientist-Astronauts by David Shayler and Colin Burgess.

In 1965, Henize heard that NASA was looking for scientists to be astronauts. The only problem was he was 37 at the time — two years older than the cutoff age. Thankfully, two years later NASA removed the age limit. Henize quickly reapplied. On August 4, 1967, Henize was one of eleven scientist-astronauts selected by NASA and the National Academy of Sciences. There were 923 applicants for that class for NASA.

Though he was accepted into the program in 1967 and began his training, Henize would have to wait 18 years to fly into space. It was a wait many of his fellow scientist-astronauts did not have the patience for, and they left the program.

"Being in the astronaut business was so much in my blood that I didn't want to get out," Henize stressed in an interview with the Cincinnati Enquirer.

Dr. Karl Henize

His excitement about space exploration didn't even waver when Henize fractured his collarbone on Sept. 27, 1968, during a physical development astronaut training class. While he did not make it to space right away, he did continue with his studies of the stars at NASA. He was among those honored by NASA Group Achievement Awards in 1971, 1974, 1975, and 1978. In 1974, he was awarded the NASA Exceptional Scientific Achievement Medal.

He was on the support crew for the Apollo 15 mission in 1971, speaking to the crew about experiments, specifically a first light flash experiment they were conducting to see if "dark-adaptations affect the visibility of flashes" which may show the flashes were caused by the retina or brain's visual cortex.

During space missions, astronauts also received wakeup calls usually in the form of songs. Henize, who was in Mission Control, decided to wake up the crew of Apollo 14 to "2001 A Space Odyssey" on Aug. 4, 1971. Henize also was the capsule communicator for Apollo 15.

According to information from NASA, during this time Henize also chaired the NASA Facility Definition Team for Starlab and chaired the NASA Working group for the Spacelab Wide-Angle Telescope. He also was chairman of the International Astronomical Union Working Group for Space Schmidt Surveys, advocating the "use of a 1-meter, all-reflecting Schmidt telescope to carry out deep full-sky (surveys) in far-ultraviolet wavelengths."

The Spacelab program would eventually take Henize to the stars. In 1985, Henize finally went into space on the Space Shuttle Challenger to help conduct SpaceLab 2 experiments.
At the time, Henize was 58 years old and would be the oldest person ever launched into space. It was a record that would later be broken by astronauts Vance Brand, Story Musgrave, John Glenn, and finally actor William Shatner, who would go into space at age 90 in 2021. Henize remains in the top ten oldest astronauts ever to go into space. Henize would oversee the payload for the mission, something he had been working on since its inception at NASA.

"In addition to the normal operations, they [the crew] would have to make many maneuvers to meet the solar and celestial viewing requirements and to deploy, fly around, and retrieve the plasma diagnostics package," according to the publication Spacelab: An International Success Story by Douglas Lord. One odd experiment, which was a departure from the rest, was to test out new can technology between Pepsi and Coca-Cola. The cans were to limit the amount of carbonation bubbles that escaped into the air.

The Spacelab 2 mission was the first to use the Spacelab Instrument Pointing System (IPS). It carried thirteen major experiments, including seven in the field of astronomy. According to NASA, Henize's responsibilities "including testing and operating the IPS, operating the Remote Manipulator System (the robotic arm to move payloads and position astronauts outside the Space Shuttle), maintaining the Spacelab systems and operating several of the experiments."

The Challenger crew was scheduled to be in space for seven days (though this would be extended for nearly another day once in orbit). After wanting to go into space since his childhood, the fact that Henize would soon be heading to the stars like Buck Rogers was thrilling. However, technical difficulties led to several delays.

On July 12, 1985, the launch countdown was stopped at T -3 seconds because of a malfunction when one of the main engine coolant valves caused a shutdown on all three engines. On July 29, the launch was delayed more than an hour and a half after a problem with a "maintenance block update." After the liftoff on July 29, there was a problem a little more than five minutes after ascent when the number one main engine shut down early, forcing the shuttle crew to do an abort to orbit. The abort meant that the intended orbit couldn't be reached but another, lower but stable orbit could be.

After returning from the mission, Henize wrote a letter to his family talking about his time in space. The Clermont Sun printed part of the letter on Oct. 2, 1985.

"It was a long wait .... But it was worth it," Henize exclaimed, later stating "the two really unique aspects of living and working in space are zero-gravity (0-G) and the mind-boggling perspective of Planet Earth you get when you circle it once every ninety minutes."

Henize went on to say that one of the most satisfying parts of his Spacelab 2 mission was "achieving most of our scientific goals in spite of several difficulties. First, we barely clawed our way into orbit after that center engine failed and this immediately upset all of our careful timelines.... Then came the initial failure of the Instrument Pointing System and one of the major experiments on it. But thanks mainly to work by ground teams (and also to a little good luck), both were operating close to normal and obtained a real bonanza of data on that final extension day."

Henize also mentioned that he suffered from what NASA called "space sickness" during the mission. He said he had a throbbing headache behind his eyes, which led to him getting sick in space. He said the headache lasted that first day and slowly got better by the second day.

"By the end of the third day I was eating well and was feeling a real sense of euphoria — living in space was really a marvelous experience!" he wrote. "Probably the greatest source of satisfaction was simply in having achieved a lifelong goal — to be among the first pioneers to venture into space and to help show the scientific value of our space capability."

During the mission, the shuttle crew released a plasma diagnostics package into an independent orbit from the shuttle. Infrared telescopes were used to obtain new readings about the heat energy of distant stars, solar telescopes looked at spots on the sun such as a giant sunspot and arcs of gas. There was an X-ray telescope gathering information on radiation from star fields in Virgo and Centaurus. There also was an electron beam gun that was used to follow natural magnetic lines to the co-orbiting plasma diagnostic package.

After the shuttle landed, Jesse Moore, who would go on to be NASA's Associate Administrator for Space Transportation, told reporters that even despite the problems it faced "Spacelab 2 returned a wealth of information. In fact, this may be the most important scientific mission that the shuttle has flown."

Henize would go on to be a member of the astronaut support crew for the Skylab 3 and 4 missions. In 1986, he retired as an astronaut to become the senior scientist in the Space Sciences Branch of NASA at Johnson Space Center (JSC). In that capacity, Henize used satellites to catalog information on space debris, which by June 1993 numbered 270 objects, according to NASA's 1999 report Orbital Debris: A Chronology. Henize used this position to track hazards to the space station and improve public awareness of space debris.

"One day, he read an article in Popular Mechanics magazine which stated that the USAF (United States Air Force) was still tracking the glove seen floating out of the Gemini 4 capsule during the EVA by Ed White in June 1965," according to the book NASA's Scientist-Astronauts. "Henize contacted the editor, pointing out that such a small object would have re-entered years before. The Air Force investigated the claim, which ironically was referred back to Henize himself at JSC as he was deemed to be the best authority in such matters. A retraction was printed in the magazine some time later."

In 1993, Henize decided to take a leave of absence from NASA to work on an experiment with High Adventure BVI, a group NASA had been consulting with regarding high-altitude parachuting research. He had gone on the trip to conduct "critical experiments," according to a press release from the Johnson Space Center. He was to conduct an experiment using a device developed by NASA to measure "the levels of radiation reaching the Earth's surface at various altitudes during the climb." He would never finish the experiment.

Henize died on Oct. 5, 1993, of high-altitude pulmonary edema (respiratory failure) as he was trying to climb Mount Everest. Per his wishes, Henize was buried on Mount Everest's Changtse Glacier. Henize was among the astronauts celebrated on

NASA Remembrance Day in 2005, honoring those "lost in the line of duty while training, experiencing their love of flight or exploration, or en route to another assignment."

In 2000, Harper College named its observatory in honor of Henize "because of his accomplishments as an astronomer and for his dedication to fulfilling his dream of reaching space."

"His name on the observatory will serve as an inspiration to the youth of today and tomorrow," the college said in a statement.

The Sky is Not the Limit: Celebrating the boundless potential of those who don the suit and helmet to venture beyond our atmosphere.

Donn Eisele

*"In the cosmos of chance, Donn Eisele's story teaches us
that sometimes, destiny is hidden in misfortune's shadow.
His journey from earthbound setbacks to celestial voyages reminds
us that the stars align not just in the skies, but also in the twists
of our lives, guiding us towards unexpected horizons."*

Sometimes, what seems like the worst luck ultimately saves your life and points you toward your destiny. Apollo astronaut Donn Eisele is the perfect example.

Eisele of Columbus was among the third group selected by NASA to be part of the Apollo program. He had an extensive background in aeronautics. Eisele held a bachelor's degree from the United States Naval Academy and received a Master of Science degree in astronautics from the Air Force Institute of Technology at Wright-Patterson Air Force Base in Dayton. He went to test pilot school and became a project engineer and experimental test pilot at the Air Force Special Weapons Center in New Mexico. It was there he filed his first of many applications for astronaut training through NASA. During his time in New Mexico, Eisele would fly experiment test flights logging 4,200 hours of flying time.

Eisele was described as a fun guy, but as a navigator he was methodical and introspective. It may have been for this reason, he along Virgil "Gus" Grissom and Ed White were selected to be part of the Apollo crew. Apollo 1 was supposed to be the first crewed Apollo mission. It was a coveted spot for the Ohioan. It must have seemed like rotten luck then when Eisele dislocated his shoulder during a zero-gravity test flight in 1965 and then again during physical activity later that year. In January 1966, he had to have shoulder surgery at Methodist Hospital in Houston. The surgery took Eisele out of flight status for weeks.

With the drive to get a man on the moon as soon as possible, it was decided to replace Eisele on the roster with Roger Chaffee. During a launch rehearsal test at Cape Kennedy, an electrical fire broke out in the cabin on January 27, 1967. Because the cabin atmosphere was pure oxygen, the fire spread incredibly quickly. The fire also created intense pressure inside the cabin, as stated by the Apollo 204 Review Board in its report on the incident.

"With a slightly higher pressure inside the Command Module than outside, opening the inner hatch is impossible because of the resulting force on the hatch," it stated. "Thus the inability of the pressure relief system to cope with pressure increase due to the fire made opening of the inner hatch impossible until after cabin rupture, and after rupture the intense and widespread fire together with rapidly increasing carbon monoxide concentrations further prevented egress."

The fire and tragic loss of three of his fellow astronauts stayed with Eisele for the rest of his life.
In his memoir Apollo Pilot: The Memoir of Astronaut Donn Eisele, he talks about the post-fire investigation that he was part of, along with fellow astronaut Walt Cunningham.

"The first thing we had to do was listen to voice tapes and try to identify who said what in the spacecraft when the fire broke out. Did you ever listen to your friends scream in panic, then agony…?" he reflected. "Listen to it over and over and over again? I don't know why we did it — I guess it seemed terribly important at the time to find out who said what."

The Apollo 204 Review Board stated they felt it was important for fellow astronauts to listen to the tapes as part of the investigation as they were "familiar with the communication systems, the crew and their voice characteristics."

The tragedy put the Apollo program on hold until NASA was certain nothing like that could happen again. A decision was made to skip Apollo 2 and 3 in the program, out of respect for the Apollo 1 crew, according to information from NASA. Apollo 4, 5, and 6 were unmanned and were used to practice maneuvers, re-entry, and the Saturn rocket.

It wasn't until 1968 when NASA decided a manned crew should take part in the program again. Apollo 1's backup astronauts were selected to be that crew. Eisele would be Apollo 7's command module pilot and would test the new digital guidance and navigation computer and systems.

"The Apollo 7 crew not only had to take over the mission that their friends and colleagues had died training for, but they had to prove to the world that the Apollo program was still in good shape to continue," stated NASA in its release on the 50th anniversary of the Apollo 7 in 2018.

While preparing for the mission, Eisele was given a new nickname. The other two astronauts on the mission with him — Walter "Wally" M. Schirra Jr. and Walter

Cunningham — jokingly referred to Eisele as "whatshisname" after several people failed to pronounce his name correctly. While pronounced Eye-sel-ee, Eisele had heard many variations over his lifetime. However, the Whatshisname moniker stuck, due to NASA Administrator Jim Web calling Eisele "Isell" when he introduced the Apollo 7 crew to President Lyndon Johnson. Eisele seemed to take the nickname in stride: In photos taken by NASA at a breakfast prior to the Apollo 7 launch Eisele used a coffee cup with "What's-his-name" written on it.

On Oct. 11, 1968, the crew of Eisele, Schirra, and Cunningham lifted off into history. In Apollo Pilot, Eisele talked about his thoughts while waiting for liftoff that morning.

"This was it," he recalled. "The moment I had been waiting for through days, months, years of preparation. I found myself thinking: Donn Eisele, air force pilot, member of the Apollo space program, astronaut, you are about to rocket into space …" Tempering that excitement were thoughts of the Greek tale of Icarus, who flew too close to the son and ended up perishing.

"Even in those ancient times men dreamed of flying yet were fearful of it," Eisele wrote, adding that what they were about to do was more fantastical than anything he had seen or read even in comic strips.

The crew would be in space for eleven days, testing out maneuvers future crews would use for the lunar mission, the performance of systems, and more. Eisele would act as navigator, with the primary task of handling and examining the guidance and navigation system.

There were some unexpected occurrences during the flight. The crew was able to fire the service module engine. While they believed it would be a smooth transition, they weren't quite prepared for the initial blast.

"We didn't quite know what to expect, but we got more than we expected," NASA reported Eisele said, adding that it felt like being plastered into their seats.

There were some technical problems as well, though none were serious. Approximately sixty-one hours into the mission, there was a malfunction in the electric power system that threatened a complete electrical shutdown, Cunningham recalled. The crews were able to fix the problem. A computer that had been combined with the telescope also locked up. Without the computer, the crew could not conduct maneuvers in orbit or have a guided re-entry. Remembering a problem that they had encountered at the MIT lab, Eisele tried what an instructor had told him, hitting the clear and adding functions to clear the program. It worked.

An unforeseen complication was that Schirra developed a head cold after the first day in space. A head cold is irritating on Earth, but in space the zero-gravity environment causes more issues. Mucus doesn't drain out and instead accumulates in the nasal passage. He had tried to blow into tissues, but that only made his eardrums hurt worse. It didn't help that Schirra couldn't rest either. The crew had a full schedule of activities and tests to perform.

Cunningham later said that "the heavy workload at the outset of the mission, combined with his discomfort, made Wally more irascible by the day. He didn't miss an opportunity to nail Mission Control to the wall … Donn and I were amazed at the patience of those in the control center with some of the outbursts that came their way. On the ground, they were well aware that every word of the air-to-ground communications was being fed directly to the press center, a fact of which we had not been informed. So Wally's bad temper was making big news back home."

A few days later, Eisele developed a runny nose, but the cold did not progress. While the colds made things difficult, the crew also found that some things were easier than expected.

"It really doesn't matter what is up or down," Eisele said, narrating the Apollo 7 Introvehicle Activity video at the Texas Archive of the Moving Image. "Even though I'm inverted [in space] there is no sense of disorientation or confusion.

"The state of being weightless actually enhances many of our abilities," Eisele explained. "It's almost like we found a new freedom."

Besides running tests on all the equipment, Eisele also was able to photograph Typhoon Gloria, which had struck the Pacific Ocean while they were in space. To keep the people back home informed and to help raise awareness and support for the space program, the three astronauts conducted 10-minute shows from orbit. The shows, which were dubbed the "The Walt, Wally and Donn Show..." were the first live American television transmission of onboard crew activities from orbit. Eisele served as narrator of the program, with Cunningham operating the camera. Schirra came in and out of the shots, sometimes holding signs.

"From the lovely Apollo Room on top of everything," was how they started the broadcast. The shows featured the astronauts talking about space flight, showing humorous signs, and "clowning around." It would go on to win a special Emmy from the National Academy of Television Arts and Sciences in 1969.

While on camera things looked happy on Apollo 7, it was not quite so easy. Schirra became a bit more irritable due to his head cold. His snapping at Mission Control and defying mission rules on re-entry (due to the cold) would later be referred to as a mutiny.

"There was some testiness involved in — you know, you can attribute whatever you want to that," said Glynn Lunney, flight director of the Apollo program. "But, it was the first time we actually had a serious falling out between the ground crew and flight crews, and it was a fracture in what had otherwise been a relatively seamless, cooperative kind of effort."

A few days before the 11th and final day in space, there was concern about re-entry with head colds. The astronauts would be unable to blow their noses with the helmets on, and it was feared that the build-up of pressure going back into the atmosphere might burst their eardrums. Mission rules dictated the helmets be worn. Schirra argued with Deke Slayton in Mission Control about the helmet issue. Schirra went against rules and told his crew to make re-entry without the helmets.

In the flight transcript, Slayton is quoted as saying, "I think you ought to clearly understand that there is absolutely no experience at all with landing without the helmet on," and later telling Schirra, "I guess you better be prepared to discuss in some detail when we land why you haven't got them on." Later Slayton would add, "the only thing we're concerned about is the landing. We couldn't care less about the re-entry. But it's your neck, and I hope you don't break it."

"Thank you, babe," Schirra replied.

"They had terrible, terrible colds," recalled Francis "Frank" Hughes, a computer and guidance, navigation, and control system expert who trained astronauts during the Apollo program. "Then the whole thing about wanting to keep their face plates up on the way home so they could clean their noses, so they could do the Valsalva (maneuver where people attempt to exhale with the nostrils and mouth closed to increase pressure in the middle ear). The only problem is he said it. He could have just been quiet and nobody would know."

The crew would each take a decongestant pill about an hour before entry, as well as not wearing helmets. All three arrived back on Earth without any problems. On October 22, 1968, Apollo 7 splashed down east of Bermuda. Eisele would log 260 hours in space during the Apollo 7 mission.
His work as a pilot on Apollo 7 was instrumental for the future of the space program.

"Eisele was a great guy to work [with]," Hughes stated. "He was the one I had worked with on the navigation on that job, so whatever we learned or dis-learned from him, it helped (Jim) Lovell even better, going through that training."

Eisele would go on to serve as the backup command module pilot for the Apollo X flight.

Later, he received the NASA Exceptional Service Medal, Air Force Senior Pilot Astronaut Wings, and the American Institute of Aeronautics and Astronautics (AIAA) Haley Astronautics Award. Eisele retired from the Air Force and left the space program in July 1972. Though he never returned to space, he created a profound legacy.

He spent two years directing the Peace Corps in Thailand after his retirement, but made sure to talk about the space program to youth at various schools. He even attended celebrations to honor the 10th anniversary of the Apollo 7 mission in Columbus in 1978. Although he left NASA, the thought of space never left Eisele. His memoir, which was not published until 30 years after his death, talks about both the good and the bad aspects of the space program.

Eisele died on Dec. 2, 1987, of a heart attack — the first of the Apollo 7 crew to die. He had been in Japan to participate in the announcement of a space camp there to teach children about space flight when he had his coronary. He was still looking toward the future of space, and his accomplishments have not been forgotten.

Eisele's ashes are buried at Arlington National Cemetery. Fellow astronaut Buzz Aldrin, who would walk on the moon in 1969 with Neil Armstrong, reflected on Eisele on what would have been his 90th birthday in June 2020.

"Remembering my dear friend Donn Eisele on what would have been his 90th Birthday. Donn served on the prime crew of Apollo 7 with my other Apollo brothers Walt Cunningham and Wally Schirra," Aldrin wrote. "Their efforts to advance American spaceflight will forever live on in future expeditions. "

Ocean of Stars: Highlighting the deep connection between the ocean's depths and the space frontier, with the boundless curiosity that drives human exploration.

Michael Gernhardt

"Michael Gernhardt merged his early passion for scuba diving and space exploration into a distinguished career. Starting as a deep-sea diver who made innovations in decompression methods, he later joined NASA, contributing significantly to shuttle missions and the ISS, and eventually played a pivotal role in lunar surface operations with Blue Origin."

Space may seem like a sea of stars. It's a comparison that joins Michael Gernhardt's two great loves.

"My first love was the ocean," Gernhardt admitted to Richland Source in 2014. His other love was space, and he was able to admire both as an astronaut and deep-sea diver.

Gernhardt was born May 4, 1956, in Mansfield, Ohio. At 10, he started scuba diving. When he reached high school, he grew very interested in both NASA's Skylab and Tektite, an underwater lab that was a multiagency program between NASA, the U.S. Navy, Department of Interior, and General Electric.

"I kind of set the distant goal that I wanted to do the most I could with the life I had, both mentally and physically, and to me, being an astronaut was the ultimate challenge in that regard," he stated.

Gernhardt graduated in 1974 from Malabar High School in Mansfield, and four years later earned his Bachelor of Science degree in physics from Vanderbilt University. He completed both his Master of Science degree and doctorate in bioengineering in 1983 and 1991, respectively, from the University of Pennsylvania.

While he was an undergraduate, Gernhardt worked as a scuba diving instructor, boat captain, and a deep-sea diver apprentice. He became a professional deep-sea diver and even developed a new theoretical decompression model — a two-way exchange of gasses to prevent decompression sickness [aka the bends] — based on tissue gas bubble dynamics.

"The discipline that it takes to do that kind of work turned out to be perfect for me when I got to NASA in terms of planning and executing spacewalks," Gernhardt stated.

Astronauts as well as divers must undergo decompression. As a professional diver, Gernhardt worked as a project engineer on a variety of subsea oil field construction and repair projects — taking part in more than 700 deep-sea dives. He also worked with the development and field implementation of new decompression tables for diving.

From 1984-88, he worked as manager and then vice president of special projects for Oceaneering International, a diving company that provides engineered products and services to engineering, defense, aerospace, entertainment, and science and research industries. In 1988, Gernhardt founded Oceaneering Space Systems, which would transfer subsea technology and operations to the International Space Station program. He worked to develop new astronaut and robot-compatible tools for space station maintenance as well as a new portable life support system and decompression procedures for EVA activities in space.

In 1992, Gernhardt was selected by NASA to join the astronaut program. He had several technical duties in addition to his space travels. He developed nitrox diving to support training for Hubble Space Telescope repair missions and EVA developments, acted as a spacecraft communicator for Mission Control, and helped lead an international research team to develop a new exercise prebreathe protocol to improve the safety and efficiency of spacewalks.

Gernhardt's first time in space was onboard Endeavour in September 1995. This was the first mission during which two different payloads were retrieved and deployed in the same mission. The payloads were the Spartan 201-003 study of the outer atmosphere of the sun and solar wind and Wake Shield Facility-2.

The mission hit a few snags before liftoff, one of which directly involved Gernhardt. A week before Endeavour was slated to fly, he tripped and dislocated his shoulder.

"I remember thinking 'this is going to be interesting,' but I had a really good attitude, which is 'I'm the best trained to do this flight and if I can do it I will, and if I can't then I'll train somebody else,'" he recalled.

Luckily, Gernhardt was still able to take part in the mission. Endeavour launched on Sept. 7, 1995. It had been postponed several times since its original launch date of Aug. 5 due to technical issues including review of nozzle joint hardware and failure of a fuel cell.

Michael Gernhardt

Among Gernhardt's responsibilities on the mission were the Wake Shield System, Spartan System, and Spartan deployment and retrieval. He took part in several spacewalks as well as detailed test objectives, many dealing with spacesuits and tools to evaluate specifics for assembly and maintenance of the space station.

Gernhardt remembered his first spacewalk where for twenty minutes one of his tasks was to go high on the robot arm in the middle of the night to try out the new glove heaters. The lights had been turned off when he was trying out the heaters.

"All the lights are out, which doesn't happen often, if ever, and I remember I can see Jupiter and its four moons with my naked eye," he recalled. "And then, I was looking down and I could see a fine line of white light on the wing of the shuttle. And then a few seconds later, a crescent of blue as the Earth was rising."

Gernhardt then was able to see St. Thomas and the Virgin Islands with Hurricane Marilyn over them.

"I had actually been a diving instructor down there. I remember looking down and seeing that hurricane and I was overcome by a great sense of pride, not for myself, but for mankind," he commented. "That we can have the technology to put me up there, you know, this great team of NASA. Here I was above the hurricane looking down from the heavens."

In addition to trying out the glove heaters, Gernhardt also assessed two of his own inventions — a body-restraint tether, which is a mechanical arm attached to the spacesuit; and a micro-conical interface, which allows robots and astronauts to remove or replace station components.

Endeavour returned to Earth on Sept. 18, 1995, after spending more than 10 days in space.

Gernhardt returned to space two years later as part of the first flight of the microgravity science laboratory on the Space Shuttle Columbia. Columbia launched on April 4, 1997, after a delay to add some additional thermal insulation to the payload. Though originally scheduled for a fifteen-day mission, the mission was cut short after a malfunction in a fuel cell once in orbit. The flight had lasted a little less than four days. Despite the short time span, crews were able to conduct some experiments, including one to observe the concentration and structure of soot from a fire in microgravity, to see under what conditions a "stable" flame ball can exist and if heat loss was involved, as well as experiments on heat and pressure tests on liquefied component bonds.

Because Columbia's flight was cut short, NASA decided to refly the mission later that year with the same crew. It was the first shuttle re-flight in NASA history.

Columbia would relaunch on July 1, 1997. It would have the same payload as before. Crews would conduct experiments as well as test hardware and procedures that would be used on ISS. Gernhardt was responsible for secondary experiments and helped with amateur radio sessions. The crew carried out more than thirty experiments during Columbia's 15-day mission.

Gernhardt would not return to space until four years later. In the meantime, NASA was setting up its Extreme Environmental Mission Operations (NEEMO), an underwater laboratory and research station 3.5 miles underwater. Gernhardt was among the first of its crew in October 2001, but he had one more space flight to complete first.

He was part of the Atlantis Shuttle crew that would attach the joint airlock module to the Unity node of ISS. The module would be called Quest. Atlantis lifted off on July 12, 2001, on its twelve-day mission. Gernhardt and the rest of the crew took several spacewalks and worked hard to attach Quest in addition to two oxygen and two nitrogen tanks used to pressurize and depressurize the airlock. Radioing down after the installation, Gernhardt thanked everyone for their hard work on the project.

"Before we conclude this EVA, Jim [Reilly] and I would both like to say thanks to the thousands of people who worked so hard to make this mission come together and be the success that it is. I'd like to tell those people they have built a very excellent airlock. Everything worked great. The spaces are much bigger than the shuttle's. It's going to add a great capability for crews to do space station maintenance," he praised.

Besides the installation, Gernhardt was responsible for the airlock systems, stowage with it, and the mission's photography and video. He also conducted Earth observations that focused on oceanography and meteorology.

Gernhardt was the principal investigator on the development and implemented a "campout" where astronauts sleep overnight in the airlock at a lower pressure. The goal of a campout is to prevent decompression sickness while astronauts work in their spacesuits, which are less pressurized than shuttles.

After returning to Earth, Gernhardt was on the first crew of NEEMO. He returned as the commander of the eighth NEEMO crew in 2005. In 2007, Gernhardt began taking part in the Pavilion Lake Research Project, which studies microbialites that live in non-extreme environments. Microbialites are underwater structures that are made up of microbes otherwise called microorganisms. He became involved in the project because it used the dual DeepWorker submersible system "as an operational analog to the dual lunar electric rover system that my team at NASA" was developing. Gernhardt actually drove one of the lunar rover prototypes during President Barack Obama's inaugural parade on Jan. 20, 2009.

Gernhardt went on to be manager of the Environmental Physiology Laboratory and principal investigator of the Prebreath Reduction Program at Johnson Space Center. His research showed that slightly elevated metabolic rates helped enhance nitrogen elimination and reduce decompression stress. He also continued to educate individuals about NASA and the sea, talking about NEEMO and how the undersea environment has helped train astronauts for long-duration missions. In 2018, he joined the board of the Divers Alert Network (DAN), a dive safety organization.

"My focus has always been to strive for safety, efficiency and simplicity in diving — whether recreational scuba instruction, commercial oilfield diving or scientific diving — and to apply those same principles to the space missions," Gernhardt said in a press release about joining the board. "I hope to use my position at DAN and its considerable expertise and professional network to promote relevant and important areas of investigation and advancements in dive safety."

Gernhardt also led a movement to develop a mission to one of the moons of Mars, Phobos. He and several others wrote papers discussing how human exploration missions to Phobos could enhance any Mars surface missions. In 2022, Gernhardt retired from NASA.

"Mike has had major contributions to human spaceflight and crew safety that have had and will continue to have a tremendous impact on us and our missions," stated Reid Wiseman, chief astronaut, in a press release about Gernhardt's retirement. "The astronaut corps will not soon forget the expertise that Gernhardt brought to NASA missions on the space station and to future missions to the moon and Mars."

During his time with NASA, Gernhardt earned four Space Flight Medals, two Exceptional Service Medals, an Exceptional Achievement Medal, and a Distinguished Service Medal.

Gernhardt continues to speak to the public about both his loves, the ocean and space. In 2023, he was one of the speakers who discussed the similarities between living under the sea and in space at the Marine Resources Development Foundation's Project Neptune.
Gernhardt now works at Blue Origin on all lunar surface operations. NASA selected Blue Origin to be a contractor to help land astronauts back on the moon. Blue Origin is building a lunar lander called the Mark 2 that is to be used during NASA's Artemis program.

Pioneer of the Infinite: Illustrating the blend of courage, dedication, and the pioneering spirit that defines the heart of an astronaut.

Nancy Currie-Gregg

*"From dreams of flight to pioneering space
and engineering frontiers, inspiring the next generation
of Mars explorers."*

You never know how the changes that happen in the world during your youth end up shaping your life. Nancy Currie-Gregg is a prime example. Currie-Gregg (aka Nancy Sherlock/Nancy Currie) was born Dec. 29, 1958, in Wilmington, Del., but considers Troy, Ohio, her hometown. Growing up she wanted to be a military aviator.

"No one told me that was not a possibility," she stated speaking at North Carolina State University in 2018. "This was before the Internet so I couldn't Google it. I did not realize that there were no female military aviators."

In the mid to late 1970s that all changed. In 1978, NASA selected its first female astronauts. Currie-Gregg said as she got older, she realized "those doors were opened for me in the nick of time."

Currie-Gregg graduated from Troy High School in 1977 and went on to receive her Bachelor of Arts degree in biological science from The Ohio State University (OSU) in 1980. She followed that with a Master of Science degree in safety engineering from the University of Southern California in 1985, and doctorate in industrial engineering from the University of Houston in 1997.

After graduating from OSU, Currie-Gregg served as a neuropathology research assistant at OSU's College of Medicine. In July 1981, she was commissioned as a second lieutenant in the U.S. Army and attended Air Defense Officer Basic Course and U.S. Army Aviation School.

While stationed at Fort Rucker, Ala., she became a helicopter instructor pilot as well as a section leader, platoon leader and brigade flight standardization officer. It was a couple of her flight students who suggested she apply for the astronaut program.

"In 1985, I applied for the astronaut program and was told that I was going to be interviewed," Currie-Gregg recalled in an interview with the ADA News. "Then in January 1986 or something like that, they canceled all the interviews. And I was called in 1987 and went down and was interviewed. I got a call and they said, "You weren't selected," and I was not surprised because I was very young. I think I was 26, 27 years old. So I thought I was severely underqualified at that point and was very young. But they followed it up immediately with, 'We want you to come work here.' I thought it was a standard rejection call until five minutes later, [when] I got a call from the senior Army officer who was an astronaut and they said, 'No, they really want you to come work here.'"

In September 1987, she became a flight simulator engineer on the shuttle training aircraft assigned to NASA's Johnson Space Center. Currie-Gregg helped develop and direct engineered flight tests. In 1990, she finally was selected by NASA to be an astronaut.

Currie-Gregg's first mission would be onboard the Space Shuttle Endeavour in 1993. Among her crewmates was fellow Ohioan G. David Low. The goal of the mission was to retrieve EURECA and use the first SPACEHAB lab. Currie-Gregg later said that every spare moment of the flight she was looking out the window.

"I can't imagine spending time doing something other than watching the sunrise on orbit," she reflected. "Every hour and a half you see a sunrise and it is the most incredible experience you have ever seen. As the sun comes up on the horizon, you just see every conceivable color painted on the horizon."

While the view was wonderful, Currie-Gregg had a lot of work to do. During the mission, her primary assignments were the EURECA system, RMS and geostationary broadcast area. In the SPACEHAB, she had several responsibilities. She used diagnostic equipment as part of a tools and diagnostic systems experiment and also conducted tests on a mock printed circuit board. Currie-Gregg communicated with Mission Control via computer messages on suggested repair procedures and results.

Later, Currie-Gregg went through a human factors assessment and set up a work platform to conduct a simulated computer procedure for a space station propulsion system. Another thing Currie-Gregg did was an impromptu plumbing job on an environmental control systems flight experiment. The experiment was a study of wastewater purification equipment. There had been a reduced flow of water through the device that required Currie-Gregg to fix it. The crew also spoke to

President Bill Clinton during the flight. Currie-Gregg thanked the president for his support of the space program.

"We all feel that the space program has done a tremendous amount for this country, both in promoting inside the country science education and also with the international partners," she stressed. "And it means a lot to us to know that, that support is still around and that we're going to have a strong space program in the future."

Currie-Gregg's next venture into space was onboard the all-Ohio flight of Discovery in 1995. The mission not only carried the tracking and data relay satellite, but several experiments. Currie-Gregg worked with the commercial protein crystal growth experiment, microgravity space tissue loss, and spoke to individuals through amateur radio. She and the rest of the crew also took part in experiments on human factors and cardiovascular effects.

"We joke in the office that we're human guinea pigs for a week or two," she said in the book To the Stars: Women Spacefarer's Legacy. "The problem is that we need the International Space Station (ISS). In ten days or fourteen days in a shuttle, you really can't get that long-term research that is required in something like biomedicine."

A few years later, Currie-Gregg saw that need fulfilled. She would be part of the first space shuttle mission to the ISS helping with its assembly in space. Endeavour launched on Dec. 4, 1998, on its eleven-day mission. The day of the launch felt momentous to Currie-Gregg.

"You walked down the same ramp that Neil Armstrong walked down when he started his day on his mission to the moon," she highlighted. "You are so well-trained and all you are thinking about is your job. But you are enormously aware of the history and those that have proceeded you."

The flight originally was to launch Dec. 3, but missed the launch window after an assessment was needed of the hydraulic system. The goal of the mission was to help with the assembly of the ISS. Currie-Gregg used the shuttle's robotic arm to join the U.S. and Russian ISS modules.
Prior to the flight, Currie-Gregg was nervous. There was only roughly 2 inches of leeway to make the module connection.

"If I miss it, you know, we may not have a space station," she said. "I mean, this is our critical piece."

The modules were able to connect on Dec. 6, 1998. There was a lot of work to do before the two modules opened onto each other, however. Crews had to attach electrical and data cables between the two modules, install handrails and other equipment to the exterior, and more.

Like most construction projects, there were some unexpected snags. Several construction items including a slidewire carrier, interface socket, pin cover, and retractable tether floated away from the orbiter, floodlights failed, and a connection was found to be incompatible between an ion exchange and hose assembly.

Finally on Dec. 10, 1998, the ISS opened. Endeavour's astronauts were able to tour the station, unstowing gear and turning on the lights. Entering ISS put Currie-Gregg in the history books as the first woman on the International Space Station.

"Definitely, without a doubt the most memorable experience of my professional life has been to be part of the crew, to enter the International Space Station for the first time and to make that call to the ground — 'Houston, this is the International Space Station,'" she exclaimed.

Her final mission into space would be aboard the Space Shuttle Columbia in March 2022. The goal of the nearly eleven-day mission was to service the Hubble Space Telescope, including the installation of the advanced camera for surveys and an experimental cryocooler. Currie-Gregg controlled the RMS several times during the mission as crews worked on the Hubble. Columbia landed on March 12. It would be the last successful landing of that vessel. In its next mission, Columbia was destroyed, re-entering the atmosphere on Feb. 1, 2003.

The Columbia disaster made Americans re-think what they believed were the dangers of space travel, Currie-Gregg said.

"Throughout my flying career, even [American] astronauts thought 99 percent of the risk was in sitting on that pad in a fully-fueled rocket and during ascent," she observed during an interview at Texas A&M University. "That's called a cognitive bias because our only accidents had happened during those times. But if we were to ask our Russian colleagues, they would have had a completely different perspective because both of their accidents happened on entry. Perspectives were completely different."

After the incident, Currie-Gregg was selected to head the Space Shuttle Program Safety and Mission Assurance Office. The office provides independent oversight and support for the space shuttle program to ensure the safety of the workforce and all NASA activities.

"A response to the Columbia accident was to establish an independent engineering organization that has our own funding," Currie-Gregg explained. "It's all within NASA but we have separate funding. We are called in to work on any major issues that any major program in NASA is [having]. Some ask for our help; some, they don't ask for our help — we decide that they need help."

She stated that the agency also worked on heat shields for the next-generation spacecraft such as the Orion.

"We call it spacecraft occupant protection, but basically, we've established crash dummy criteria for spacecraft occupants, just like with cars," she stated.

In addition to the assurance office, Currie-Gregg also served in other capacities at NASA following her fourth space flight. She was the manager of the habitability and human factors office, a senior technical advisor in NASA's Automation, Robotics and Simulation Division and chief engineer for the organization's engineering and safety center. Currie-Gregg retired as a colonel in the U.S. Army in May 2005. In 2017, she retired from NASA.

Pat Forrester, chief of the astronaut office at Johnson Space Center, praised Currie-Gregg for her contributions "not just to the astronaut office and the Johnson Space Center but to the entire agency."

During her time at NASA, Currie-Gregg earned several honors, including the Outstanding Leadership Award, Presidential Ranking Award, and four Space Flight Medals. She also was recognized with the QASAR Safety Award, Exceptional Service Medal, Flight Simulation Engineering Award, Silver Snoopy Award, two Defense Superior Service Medals, Legion of Merit, two Defense Meritorious Service medals, and the Silver Order of St. Michael Army Aviation Award.

Her accomplishments have placed her in the Army Aviation Association Hall of Fame; Delaware Aviation Hall of Fame; Women in Aviation, International Pioneer Hall of Fame; Ohio Veterans Hall of Fame; Ohio Hall of Fame; the and Ohio State University Army ROTC Hall of Fame. The observatory at Enid High School is named in her honor as well.

After her retirement, Currie-Gregg went into teaching at Texas A&M. She continues to be a professor of engineering practice, industrial and systems engineering, and aerospace engineering. She continues to research aerospace and how it affects humans, as well as spacecraft occupant protection, human-robot interaction, and systems safety engineering. Currie-Gregg said that many of her students still ask her about space and what it was like being an astronaut.

"That's really the joy of it, sharing my experiences and hopefully to inspire the future engineers and hopefully even the future astronauts for this country and hopefully out of Texas A&M University," she beamed.

Currie-Gregg said with the private sector entering space, it will be interesting to see what happens in the future.

"I think ultimately for most people inside the agency, [and] I think for the public, ... the ultimate goal is Mars," she pointed out. "My class patch has the moon and Mars on it, because the first President Bush said we were going to go back to the moon and on to Mars, and we thought we were the astronauts that were going to do it. [But] we weren't it. I used to say that there's a school kid somewhere today who's going to be the first one to set foot on Mars, and I certainly hope that's the case. I certainly hope to see it in my lifetime."

Honor and Achievement: An accolade to the decorated career of a spacefarer celebrating his extraordinary contributions to space exploration.

Robert Overmyer

"Robert 'Buck' Overmyer, a true pioneer from Ohio to orbit, reminds us that the journey to the stars is a blend of brilliance, bravery, and the unexpected. His story, soaring from earthly trials to space triumphs, echoes the adventurous spirit of Buck Rogers, bridging the gap between childhood dreams and cosmic realities."

From Apollo to the space shuttles, Ohioan Robert Overmyer saw it all as part of the space program. The Marine Corps veteran was considered an integral part of the space shuttle program.

While born in Lorain, Overmyer considered Westlake — where he grew up and graduated high school — his hometown. Growing up, Overmyer's family nicknamed him "Buck" — like Buck Rogers — because of his interest in space, which would only grow as he got older.

Overmyer received a Bachelor of Science degree in physics from Baldwin Wallace College in 1958, then a Master of Science degree in aeronautics from the U.S. Naval Postgraduate School in 1964. Between earning his two degrees, Overmyer entered active duty with the Marine Corps, serving with the Marine Attack Squadron 214 in 1959. He then served with the Marine Maintenance Squadron 17, before being assigned to the Air Force Test Pilots School. Ever interested in space, he took part in the Air Force's Manned Orbiting Laboratory Program before it was canceled. Overmyer earned the Air Force's Meritorious Service Medal in 1968 for his duties with that program.

In 1969, he was selected as an astronaut by NASA. From the time of his selection until 1971, Overmyer was involved in the engineering development of the Skylab program, which had a goal "to prove that humans could live and work in space for extended periods" while expanding knowledge of astronomy. It was a program he would work with several times during his career as an astronaut.

In November 1971, he was a member of the support crew for Apollo 17, assigned as the launch capsule communicator. In 1973 until mid-1975, he was part of the support crew for the Apollo-Soyuz Test project, acting as the NASA capsule communicator in the Mission Control Center in Moscow.

He would be awakened early one morning in July 1975, when there were concerns about a piece of hardware on the mission.

"[They] wanted a total briefing on what the trouble was and what could be done to correct it," Overmyer said at the time. "That's what we're here for."

In 1976, he was reassigned, this time to duties on the Space Shuttle Approach and Landing Test program, which was a series of taxi and flight trials of a prototype space shuttle. Overmyer was awarded the Marine Corps Meritorious Service Medal in 1978 for his work as a chief chase pilot and as a support crewman for the shuttle approach program. In 1979, Overmyer was made deputy vehicle manager of the Columbia Space Shuttle and placed in charge of finishing the manufacturing and tiling of that vessel. Richard Nygren, who worked with NASA's Flight Crew Support Division, said that Overmyer was called the "tile czar" and oversaw "all of the tile work" at Kennedy Space Center. He would have that duty until Columbia went to the launch pad in 1980.

It wasn't until 1982 that Overmyer would take his turn among the stars as part of Columbia's first fully operational flight. He was named pilot of the mission. Other crew members included commander Vance Brand and mission specialists Joseph Allen and Wiliam Lenoir.

The five-day mission launched on Nov. 11, 1982. In addition to being the first operational flight, Columbia's crew were to deploy two commercial communication satellites. The mission also was to include the first space walk, but hardware failures in both spacesuits prevented that from happening. Three experiments were conducted onboard as well.

The crew received a very special phone call in space on the first day of the mission. President Ronald Reagan called to congratulate them on a great start. On Nov. 16, the shuttle would touch down to applause from Mission Control.

"We deliver," Brand stated as the shuttle landed. "Nice to be back."

The phrase "we deliver" became a calling card for the crew. In December 1982, Overmyer spoke at the City Club of Cleveland about the flight.

"I feel a great honor to represent NASA and to have represented Cleveland and Ohio in the space shuttle," he stated.

Overmyer said that in late fall 1981 he was told about being on the crew.

"We were told we would fly the first four-man crew of the shuttle. We had a very basic job to do. We were to launch safely, get into orbit and deploy two commercial satellites, and to return and land safely. If we did that, we would accomplish 100 percent of our mission. We were the proof of concept of the shuttle," he stated.

The shuttle ride "was quite a thrill" he exclaimed, adding he was glad to have his opportunity in space "after finally seeing so many of my friends and contemporaries go, it was my turn. ... I am personally really proud to be part of the 'we deliver' crew."

Overmyer would next head to space three years later on the Space Shuttle Challenger. Between the two missions, he received the U.S. Naval Postgraduate School Distinguished Engineer Award, USMC Distinguished Flying Cross, and the NASA Space Flight Medal for his work. Still, his biggest challenges were yet to come.

Overmyer acted as commander of the 1985 Challenger mission. He commanded a crew consisting of four astronauts and two payload specialists. The 1985 Challenger expedition was the second flight of the Spacelab module, designed to conduct a series of experiments including those involving material and life sciences, fluid mechanics, astronomy, and physics. Crews grew "improved" crystals in space that would be used in technological devices. The effects of weightlessness also were examined in two monkeys and twenty-four rodents that were onboard.

The mission lasted seven days. The flight lifted off on April 29, 1985, after a two-minute delay due to a launch-processing system error. It would be the first of several issues on the flight.
Astronaut John Fabian said the Challenger flight had a few challenges, one of which involved the cages the monkeys were kept in.

"These were claimed to be totally recycling the air inside and no offshoot of any type of contaminants from inside," he recalled. "And when those cages flew their first time, it was on a flight with Bob Overmyer, and there was monkey crap floating around all over the place."

Overmyer definitely wasn't happy, especially when some of the feces ended up in the cockpit of the space shuttle — twenty-five feet away from the cages.

"Feces in the cockpit isn't all that much fun, guys," Overmyer complained to Mission Control. "That really has me concerned. If we have monkey feces up here, we surely don't have any health [sanitation] up in this area." Later Overmyer could be heard talking during cabin communications.

"How many years did we tell them those cages weren't going to work?" he lamented. "That's really discouraging if we're going to get monkey feces up here. Son of a gun."

The crew ended up wearing surgical masks until filters cleared the air of any droppings. Crew members also had to come up with solutions for several problems on the flight, such as there being no fresh water from their galley faucet (they bypassed the faucet using an all-purpose hose) and a faulty urine collection device.

Despite the issues, Overmyer and his crew completed a successful mission, with fourteen out of the fifteen primary Spacelab experiments deemed a success. The crew also deployed two satellites during the flight, which ended on May 6, 1985.

Overmyer would have a lot more involvement with Challenger, but not in any way he or NASA had hoped. Eight months after his flight on the vessel, the Challenger spacecraft would break apart in what looked like an explosion on Jan. 28, 1986, killing all onboard. Overmyer was among those tasked by NASA with investigating Challenger's demise.

While dealing with the heartbreak of losing his colleagues and looking into the cause, Overmyer stumbled upon something that must have shaken him deeply. He found that the issue that caused Challenger to break apart had emerged during his 1985 flight on the same vessel. Overmyer's crew had come within less than a second of dying as the result of an O-ring issue, according to one engineer's estimate. It was not the only knowledge that would affect him deeply.

During the investigation, Overmyer would be there as the wreckage of the cabin was found and brought to shore. There were reports that some of the remains of crew members were inside. Despite many believing Challenger's crew died instantly, Overmyer did not.

Overmyer had been close friends with Challenger's commander Col. Dick Scobee, with whom he co-owned a plane. Overmyer firmly believed that the crew was alive after Challenger broke apart and Scobee tried to save his crew members in the crew cabin.

"Scob fought for any and every edge to survive," Overmyer said. "He flew that ship without wings all the way down."

Later in 1986, Overmyer retired from both NASA and the U.S. Marine Corps. No reason was given for his retirement, according to reports. He retired a colonel. After leaving NASA, Overmyer worked for McDonnell Douglas to help design a space station. He later would be a test pilot for Cirrus Design Corp. On March 22, 1996, he was testing a prototype when the plane suddenly went down near Duluth, Minn. Overmyer was killed in the crash.

He was laid to rest in Arlington National Cemetery. He later was inducted into the Ohio Department of Veteran Services' Hall of Fame in 1993. In 2014, an Ohio Historical Marker was erected at Clague Memorial Park in Westgate in his memory. During its dedication ceremony, Overmyer's widow, Kitty, was on hand. She said her husband would have been proud to be remembered in the community where he grew up.

Liftoff to History: Commemorating his collaborative spirit of space exploration, with excitement and a unity of shared purpose.

Kenneth Cameron

*"Kenneth Cameron, a visionary in space exploration,
epitomizes the journey from earthly soldier to cosmic diplomat.
His life, an odyssey from the battlegrounds of Vietnam
to the frontier of space, underlines a profound transition:
from the competition of the Cold War to the collaboration in space.
Cameron's tale is a testament to the power of curiosity and education,
proving that a soldier's discipline and an astronaut's dream
can coalesce into a legacy that transcends borders,
both terrestrial and celestial."*

With the Cold War ending in the late 1980s, a new era of cooperation began on a global scale. While the U.S. and Russia had been engaged in the space race prior, they had worked together at times. Now, a truly international effort would strive to advance science and technology across the globe. Astronaut Kenneth Cameron was at the center of much of that cooperation.

Cameron was born in Cleveland. He graduated from Rocky River High School in Ohio in 1967 before going to Massachusetts Institute of Technology (MIT). He left after two years to enlist in the US. Marine Corps during the Vietnam Conflict in 1969. While there are several things he remembers about his start in the Marines, one memory stands out.

"I was in boot camp when these guys came into the mess hall and announced two Americans just walked on the moon in July 1969," he recalled during an event at Johnson Space Center. "I thought I'd better get busy then."

In 1970, Cameron would do one tour of duty in Vietnam and later would be part of the Maine security guards at the U.S. Embassy in Saigon. He would return to the United States and in 1972 would go into flight training. Cameron received his aviation wings in 1973.

During his military career he would earn a Legion of Merit, Defense Superior Service Medal, two Distinguished Flying Crosses, a Navy Commendation Medal with a Combat V, Combat Action ribbons, a Vietnamese Meritorious Unit Citation, and a Marine Corps Association Leadership Sword.

In 1976, Cameron was able to return to MIT through its Marine College Degree and Advanced Degree Program. He would earn a research fellowship at the C.S. Draper Laboratory, studying technical areas in engineering and sciences. Cameron has often said that the flights of Alan Shephard and John Glenn inspired him to pursue flight as well as education in science and technology.

Glenn's inaugural orbit around the Earth inspired Cameron to follow in his footsteps, and going to MIT made him feel that he could become an astronaut.

"I realized as an aviator and an MIT graduate, I actually had a shot," he said.

Cameron would receive a Bachelor of Science degree in aeronautics and astronautics from MIT in 1978, earning a Master of Science degree a year later from MIT in the same area of study. In addition, Cameron would take several Russian language courses, which would prove very beneficial in his career.

"I was back in school training to be an engineer and they said I had to take some humanities classes," he stated. "I realized all those Russian airplanes I was studying — everything inside was Russian so I'd be a little better off if I could speak Russian. I studied ... and years later NASA was looking for someone with that training."

After graduating from MIT, Cameron headed to the U.S. Navy Test Pilot School, where he graduated in 1983. Cameron became a test pilot at the Naval Air Test Center, flying in 48 different types of aircraft. With his test-flight experience, Cameron applied to NASA to see if he could follow in the footsteps of the space explorers who inspired him in his youth.

"There is no one path to get to NASA," he stressed. "I'd liked what I was doing but wanted another challenge."

Cameron was selected to be an astronaut in 1984. Besides training, Cameron would use his education to work on several different projects, including a tethered satellite payload, flight software testing for the Shuttle Avionics Integration Laboratory, and more. He helped with support activities at both Kennedy Space Center and Mission Control. He was a member of NASA when the Challenger disaster happened in 1985.

Cameron said losing the Challenger "was a tremendous setback" to the space program.

"The key to one's character is how we respond to setbacks," he continued. "We lost a certain amount of innocence but we now have a lot more strength and directed energy."

Cameron knew all the astronauts who were lost in the Challenger disaster personally, as they had worked together in the same Houston office. While NASA worked on issues with the shuttle, there was never any question in Cameron's mind that manned flights would return.

"Certain things can only be done by a crew," Cameron explained. "The real value with humans aboard is that we can do almost everything. However, we have to decide how important it is just for a ride by an observer, given the risk involved."

While the space shuttle program returned in 1988, Cameron would have to wait three more years for his chance to go to space. His parents, Ginny and Donald, would be on hand to watch his first mission in 1991 on the Space Shuttle Atlantis. The flight would be responsible for the deployment of the Gamma Ray Observatory, which would look for gamma ray sources in the universe. The observatory would change the world's knowledge of the sky. There would be other experiments during the mission, including studies in biomedical material processing, growing crystals, an amateur radio experiment, and radiation monitoring.

Atlantis launched on April 5, 1991, and orbited for six days. During the orbit Cameron and other astronauts used a ham radio to talk to school children, amateur radio operators, and cosmonauts from Mir. Cameron also acted as the pilot on the mission. He monitored the progress of spacewalks, and helped with the deployment of the observatory, which proved very beneficial to science. It would find new classes of galaxies powered by black holes, as well as gamma rays from Earth's thunderstorms.

On his first flight, Cameron didn't find weightlessness to be a problem. Getting accustomed to gravity upon his return was another story — even after later flights.

"You've probably seen all the pictures of astronauts playing with their food in orbit or enjoying the weightless environment while they eat," Cameron acknowledged in a video for MIT alumni. "Once back on the ground, in the van where they take you back to crew quarters, I was drinking orange juice. I poured a glass of orange juice for myself and the person [sitting close to me]. I passed the orange juice to them and just released [it], pushing it toward him. It would have worked perfectly in orbit. It made a great mess there so there's a lot of accommodation you have to go through getting back."

Cameron's second mission was in 1993 onboard the Space Shuttle Discovery. The shuttle, of which Cameron was commander, carried ATLAS-2. ATLAS stands for

Atmospheric Laboratory for Applications and Science. The lab had seven experiments which would be used to examine atmospheric and solar conditions "to better understand the effect of solar activity on the Earth's climate and environment." The crew also would deploy and retrieve the Spartan solar physics satellite to observe the Sun's corona.

Getting Discovery off the ground to conduct the experiments proved a little troublesome. The shuttle had a limited window to launch so crew members could observe seasonal changes (going from spring to summer) in the northern hemisphere. At T -9 minutes on April 6, the launch was put on hold when a higher-than-expected temperature was detected on an engine valve. After an hour, the clock started again. The countdown then stopped at T -11 seconds because of an instrument error. The launch was rescheduled to April 8.

Thankfully, everything went well on this launch. The spacecraft would be in orbit for nine days. After his second space flight, Cameron would go to Moscow in 1994 as the first NASA director of operations in Star City, which is a training center for cosmonauts. He would receive Russian training in Soyuz and Mir spacecraft systems. He also would have flight training in a Russian L-39 aircraft.

The training was beneficial for Cameron's next flight. He would return to the United States to command the Space Shuttle Atlantis in 1995. The mission would be the second docking of a U.S. space shuttle to the Russian Space Station Mir. The shuttle launched in November 1995 on an eight-day mission.

The Atlantis crew would focus on delivering a Russian-built docking module to Mir to assist with better links between Mir and space shuttles. Cameron would maneuver Atlantis to help connect the dock to the space station. With the docking module in place, hatches between the two space vessels could be opened with crews transferring between the two. Cameron was the one who pulled open the hatch separating the spaceships. After opening the hatch, Cameron reportedly greeted the commander of Mir with a box of chocolates.

"Part of building and working together is building friendships," Cameron said. "We want to build an international space station in the future, and we start by building friendships between people."

The shuttle crew brought other gifts including maple candy, ice cream sandwiches, and a guitar with headphones, as well as needed lithium hydroxide canisters to help with any faulty environmental systems. On the sixth day of the mission, crews received a call from United Nations (UN) Secretary General Boutros Boutros-Ghali, who commented on the 50th anniversary of the United Nations and noted the UN's flag on the mission.

"We are very pleased that you have seen the United Nations flag flying behind this international crew, along with the flags of each of the nations and organizations which have sponsored this mission," Cameron declared on the call. "This flag was launched to the space station Mir onboard the Soyuz and will be returned to Earth aboard the Space Shuttle Atlantis.... We hope this gesture of transferring a United National flag from a Russian space station to an International Space Station and returning to Earth on the space shuttle will help commemorate the international nature of this venture and the future that we have in space together."

Atlantis would undock from Mir on Nov. 18 before heading back to Earth two days later. Before leaving Mir, Atlantis' crew would affix their crew patch to the bulkhead of the station.

Cameron left NASA in 1996 to work in the private industry. He worked at Hughes Training, Inc., Saab Automobile, and at General Motors Technical Center.

Everything changed after the Columbia Space Shuttle disaster on Feb. 1, 2003. Columbia broke apart while re-entering the atmosphere. The cause of the destruction was a piece of foam insulation that broke off the propellant tank and damaged the shuttle's wing. All seven astronauts onboard were killed. It was the second space shuttle disaster in the program after Challenger.

Cameron returned to NASA in 2003, securing a founding position at the NASA Engineering and Safety Center (NESC). The center is dedicated to proactively aiding NASA by performing independent testing, analysis, and assessment of high-risk projects "to ensure safety and mission success." In his new post, Cameron was a principal engineer and later became the deputy director for safety. In December 2008, Cameron retired from NASA again.

During his time at NASA, Cameron earned several honors, including the NASA Leadership Medal, NASA Exceptional Achievement Medal, and three space flight medals. Cameron continues to encourage space travel and speak to those interested in aviation. In 2023, he took part in several "Meet the Astronaut of the Day" events at Kennedy Space Center. He has also spoken to students in Ohio and elsewhere, urging them to dream of the future.

"Someone out there may one day be the next astronomer, physicist, medical researcher, or scientist in space," Cameron encouraged students at his alma mater of Rocky River High School in 1986.

Cameron encouraged curiosity in youth during a STEM event in 2015.

"When you look out the window at the Earth you are looking at a spaceship with 5 billion crew members going 66,000 miles around the sun.... It is a spaceship and in order for it to continue being a good spaceship, it takes a lot of people understanding how it works," he stated. "That takes people who are young being curious about how things work. ... How things work and being curious is key to understanding how the spaceships work. Once you know how it works you can make it better and that's how we can make the world better. We're all astronauts but have different spaceships."

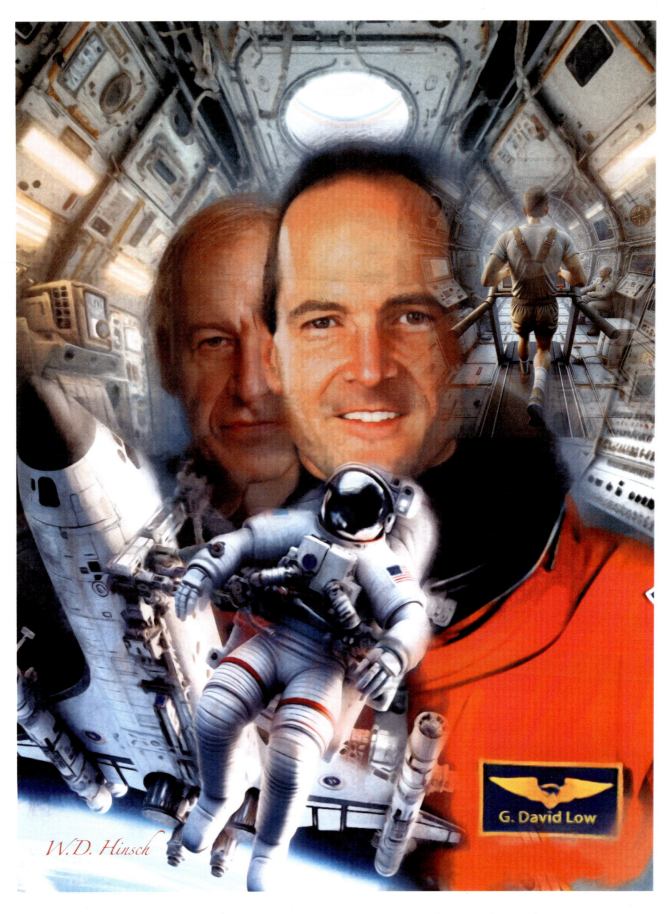

Layers of Legacy: Showcasing an astronaut's journey, from earthy confines of technology to the weightlessness of space.

G. David Low

*"In a life intertwined with the stars, G. David Low
transformed from a son of NASA's 'ultimate engineer' to
a pioneering astronaut himself. Navigating his journey from
academic brilliance to spaceflight ingenuity, Low's legacy orbits
not just around his own stellar achievements but also in inspiring future
voyages beyond our world. His story, a testament to
curiosity and dedication, reminds us that the cosmos
is not just a frontier to explore,
but a legacy to uphold."*

G. David Low grew up with the space program — literally. Low, who was born in Cleveland in 1956, was the son of Mary and George M. Low. His father was NASA deputy administrator from 1969-76 and was called the "ultimate engineer." He had been integral to the lunar missions of the Apollo program.

"Ever since I was selected as an astronaut candidate I have been asked whether my father's involvement in the space program was behind my interest in becoming an astronaut," Low said in an interview after his NASA selection. "I am sure that being so close to the space program for the first twenty years of my life because of my father's connection with it had to have some effect on me. On the other hand, I cannot say with any degree of certainty that I would not have developed this same interest had my father not been involved in the program at all. I only know that I am extremely excited about this opportunity."

Low graduated from Langley High School in Virginia in 1974. He went on to receive a Bachelor of Science degree in physics and engineering from Washington and Lee University in 1978, followed by a Bachelor of Science degree in mechanical engineering in 1980 from Cornell University.

From 1980-84, Low worked in the California Institute of Technology's Jet Propulsion Laboratory. He was involved in the lab's spacecraft systems engineering section, where he helped plan several planetary missions as well as systems engineering designs for spacecraft. One such spacecraft was the Galileo, which launched in 1989 with the goal of studying Jupiter. He also was the principal spacecraft systems engineer for the Mars Observer spacecraft, which launched in 1992 to study the surface of Mars.

Low took time off from the lab to pursue his Master of Science degree in aeronautics and astronautics, which he received from Stanford University in 1983. In 1984, he was selected to be an astronaut by NASA. Low was the youngest in his astronaut class, being 28 years old. He was one of seventeen candidates selected from 4,934 applications. His father was able to see his son accepted into the astronaut program just prior to the senior Low's death in 1984. When he was selected as an astronaut candidate, Low knew it may be years before he would make it to space.

"I know that seems a long, long way off right now," he reflected. "But there is a lot of exciting work to be done along the way, and I can't wait to get started on it."

Before going into space, Low performed several technical duties for NASA. He would work on the Canadarm, as well as extravehicular activity (EVA) and Orbiter tests at Kennedy Space Center. He also served as the spacecraft communicator at Mission Control for four flights. In 1986, he took part in an escape test for the shuttle program.

Fellow astronaut Frank Culbertson said that Low was "more academic than the rest of us."

"He also became a very good operator," Culbertson said. "He was good with his hands, a good mechanic who worked on cars, but he understood the physics behind everything. He also was a good communicator."

Low's first space flight was onboard the Columbia, which launched on Jan. 9, 1990. The launch had several delays because of work to finish an overhaul of the launch pad and weather concerns. It was a ten-day mission, during which Low literally ran around the world getting his work done. Commander Daniel Brandenstein praised Low, who acted as a mission specialist, for his work ethic.

"G. David was a very dedicated, smart guy," he stated in the book Space Shuttle Stories. "He was the first person to run around the world; he got on the treadmill one day and ran for an orbit. Then we had a big piece of teleprinter paper that we held across the middeck, which he broke through as he completed the run. He was a good guy."

Low was a bit nervous for his first space mission. During an interview with United Press International, Low spoke about going on his initial flight.

"I guess I'll be very, very happy if we can get the wheels stopped and I haven't screwed anything up," Low uttered. "That'll be a tremendous relief, to go through ten days and know that I did it right."

When asked what he was most looking forward to in space, Low simply stated, "Just looking out the window."

Low also brought something special along for his first flight: a pair of tan, silk socks that had been worn by Cornell University's founder Ezra Cornell. Cornell had worn the socks on his wedding day in 1831.

The mission wasn't all fun. Its goal was to launch a Navy communications satellite and retrieve the Long Duration Exposure Facility.

"If we don't grab it, it's a total loss of all the data and there's a lot of very good data on board ... that can be used directly in designing things such as the space station," Low explained at the time.

During the mission, Low was responsible for launching the Syncom communication satellite and conducting as well as participating in medical experiments designed to tell more about how humans adapt to weightlessness. Low felt the medical experiments were vital to the future of human space travel.

"There are people who want, for scientific reasons, to fly longer duration missions," Low stressed. "They've mentioned sixteen days, they've mentioned twenty-eight days, and they want to do it with the space shuttle prior to getting the space station operational.... What we're doing with this mission, we're sort of a precursor to the EDO (extended duration orbiter) missions, beginning to build a better medical database.

"There are certain questions we have to have answered before we can commit to having a pilot and a commander try to fly ... back after long durations in space," Low said. "You don't want to have a commander or a pilot on a sixteen-day mission to come back and black out because of the onset of [gravity]."

Low's first mission also hit one important milestone. At nearly eleven days long, it set a new shuttle endurance record. Low's next flight would be in 1991, onboard Space Shuttle Atlantis. The nine-day mission would see the crew deploying a tracking and data relay satellite and additional experiments relating to EDO missions.

The launch faced several delays. It was originally scheduled for July 23, but a faulty controller on one of the main engines needed to be replaced. On Aug. 1, 1991, the launch was halted at T -9 minutes when a vent valve would not indicate it was closed. Finally, on Aug. 2, Atlantis launched.

Low ran tests on a portable computer that was used for experiments on systems being examined for use on the space station. He and fellow astronaut Michael Baer also tested out a vacuum sack (a waist-high collapsible container) designed to ease light-headedness space travelers experience upon their return to Earth. It was another experiment designed to aid in longer space trips. Low had to climb into the sack, but there were some issues. There was trouble getting the seal of the container to fit tightly around his waist. Crews even shoved towels between Low and the sack to get a tighter fit. They eventually had to pull the belt of the sack up to his torso to get a tighter fit. Mission Control joked with Low, telling him he could take a light snack into the sack.

"I'll take a Big Mac and a chocolate shake," he jested.

Once inside the sack, Low's legs and hips were subjected to lower atmospheric pressure, which helped to pull blood back to his legs and reduce the stress on his heart. Echocardiography images of Low's heart were taken during the procedure.

"We think that by emphasizing that, we might be able to have the body readapt to the [gravity] environment in a quicker fashion upon return to Earth," Low said prior to the launch.

The vacuum sack and other experiments were to help astronauts undertake longer missions in anticipation of the International Space Station.

"If the data that we accumulated is only as good as the time we had collecting it, we'll certainly push back the frontiers of technology," Low stated.
Though a veteran of two space flights, Low wasn't done learning everything he could about the space program. NASA decided to build up the astronauts' experience base on extravehicular activities in 1992. Low and many other NASA employees would spend hours working, as NASA put it, "to refine training methods for spacewalks, expand the EVA experience levels of astronauts, flight controllers, and instructors, and aid in better understanding the difference between true microgravity and the ground simulations used in training."

A year later, Low would take his final space flight on the Space Shuttle Endeavour. The shuttle would launch on June 21, 1993. During the mission, Low and fellow astronaut Jeff Wisoff would conduct a nearly six-hour spacewalk to work on a communications antenna on the EURECA (European Retrievable Carrier, which carried several experiments and solar observations) and to work on fine alignment tests. He and other crew members also worked on EVAs to test out tools and techniques for future missions.

The mission also had a module known as SPACEHAB, which supported NASA's commercial development of the space program by providing more than double the pressurized workspace needed for experiments tended to by crew members. The experiments inside SPACEHAB included ones on drug improvement, feeding plants, soldering, cell splitting, and more. There also were experiments on board dealing with biotechnology, crystal growth, and microgravity.

Though his last trip to space was in 1993, Low worked for NASA for several years after his last mission. He was part of the Russian integration team that helped coordinate the transition from Mir-2/Space Station Freedom to the International Space Station. He then worked as the manager of the EVA office in NASA's legislative affairs office. Low would act as a direct liaison with the U.S. Congress on NASA's aerospace programs. During his time at NASA, Low earned three NASA Space Flight Medals, the NASA Exceptional Service Medal, and NASA's Outstanding Leadership Medal.

Low left NASA in 1996 to join Orbital Sciences, which designed, manufactured, and launched space and launch vehicles for commercial, military, and government customers. There he managed safety measures and later their commercial space transportation program, becoming a senior vice president. Low was called "an extraordinarily inspiring and thoughtful leader, extremely talented engineer, and a courageous space explorer," by Orbital's staff. Under his leadership, the company became a partner with NASA and was awarded a contract to resupply the International Space Station with various equipment, supplies, and payloads.

Low did not live to see the company's first flight to the station; he died of cancer in 2008. He was 52. In 2013, Orbital Science Corp. (now Northrop Grumman Space Systems) christened its first commercial cargo spacecraft after Low.

"Orbital has a tradition going back twenty-five years or more of naming many of our launch vehicles and spacecraft, and we're going to continue that tradition on this one," Frank Culbertson, Orbital's executive vice president and a former NASA astronaut, told reporters. "We are very proud to name the spacecraft 'G. David Low' and carry this tradition and honor him in this way into space."

Culbert stressed that the ship, the G. David Low, was named to "reflect a real pioneer of the space program, particularly at Orbital."

Defying Gravity: Capturing the essence of adventure, reflecting the boldness of those Who have soared above the Earth, pushing the boundaries of what's possible.

Robert Springer

*"Robert Springer's story, emerging from
a small town in Ohio to traverse the vast expanse of space,
is a vivid illustration of a life driven by bravery and inquisitiveness.
His guiding principle of grasping every chance echoes far beyond
astronautics, capturing a fundamental truth: it is through audacity and
steadfast determination that we chart our path to the stars and return.
His narrative, interweaving military gallantry with the quest of space
exploration, stands as a powerful reminder of the limitless
capabilities inherent in all of us to ascend to new
peaks and venture into the unknown."*

Astronaut Robert Springer has one piece of advice for people, no matter their age. "One of the things I try to emphasize is to take advantage of the opportunities that are out there," he stressed. "They are everywhere. You have to be bold enough and strong enough to go in and seek out those opportunities and make the most of them."

Springer knows a lot about seizing opportunities. Though he was born in St. Louis, Mo., Springer considers Ashland, Ohio, his hometown. He grew up there, graduating from Ashland High School in 1960. Springer said he didn't always want to be an astronaut for one important reason: "When I was a real youngster — 4-5 years old — there weren't any astronauts."

After high School, Springer received his Bachelor of Science degree in naval science from the United States Naval Academy, followed by a Master of Science degree in operations research and systems analysis from the U.S. Naval Postgraduate School. Springer completed his flight training and received his aviator wings in 1966. He would go on to fly F-4 aircrafts, completing 300 combat missions in Vietnam. In 1968, he served as an advisor to the Republic of Korea's Military Corps in Vietnam. During that time, he flew 250 helicopter missions. He went on to attend the Navy Fighter Weapons School (Top Gun). There was more pilot training to come.

In 1975, he graduated from the U.S. Navy Test Pilot School and would go on to test pilot more than twenty types of aircraft. He eventually graduated from Armed Forces Staff College and assumed responsibility for joint operational planning for Marine forces in NATO and the Middle East.

During his time in the military, he received the Defense Distinguished Service Medal, Legion of Merit, Navy Distinguished Flying Cross, Bronze Star, Navy Achievement Medal, Combat Action Ribbon, Presidential Unit Citation, Navy Unit Citation, and various Vietnam campaign ribbons.
He had earned various military honors and was enjoying his military career when he learned NASA was looking for astronauts.

"When NASA started accepting applicants for the first shuttle pilots and mission specialists in the 1970s, I had a good friend that I had gone to graduate school with and was an Army officer come to my house one Saturday morning," Springer recalled. "[He] said 'well you know NASA's announced they are going to be accepting astronaut candidates. Are you going to do that?' I said I hadn't given it that much thought. He said 'well you've got all the credentials' and handed me a stack of papers. He said 'there's the application. Sign it and send it in.' I ended up getting selected. It was kind of a bold step."

Springer spoke a lot about his space experience in 2022 in Ashland during the Ashland County Historical Society's Speaker Series. He called the interview process to become an astronaut the "most interesting job interview in my life." A panel of astronauts interviewed candidates and had asked him what he would do if he was not selected by NASA.

"I was honest," he explained. "It hadn't been a long-term career plan for me. I said 'I really enjoy what I'm doing today. If I don't get — I want to get selected — but if I don't I'll go back doing what I've been doing as a Marine and as a pilot.'"

Springer was selected in May 1980 to join NASA. He would serve as support crew for STS-3 (Columbia Space Shuttle's third test flight), participate in concept development studies for the space operations center, and work on final development of the remote manipulator system. He also worked in the Mission Control Center for seven flights between 1984-85.

Springer said there is a lot of teamwork when it comes to space travel and NASA. "Everyone has a job but when someone needs help you reach across and help," he stressed.

Training was going well and Springer was preparing for his first flight when the Challenger disaster happened in 1986. The flight carried astronauts who were admitted in the same year he was. The pilot, Francis Scobee, was his close friend.

"That was a personal loss for me," Springer reflected. "The pilot of the Challenger was my best friend in the program. I knew his family and kids. It made it doubly difficult. I get asked this question often — did anyone quit [the program after Challenger]? Did anyone lose their resolve? The answer is not one person did. We, in fact, we all doubled down and said we are going ... it took us three years to get back into it."

Because of his degrees, Springer spent a lot of time at Rockwell International, which manufactured the space shuttle.

"We made over 200 major changes in the program" after Challenger, Springer stated.

It would take nearly three years for NASA to launch another shuttle. Springer would have his first space flight on the 1998 Discovery Space Shuttle.

"This was a culmination of nine years of training because of the three years delay [of Challenger]," Springer explained. "Our primary job on this flight was to deploy the tracking relay data satellite."

Discovery would launch on March 13 and would be a five-day mission. In addition to the satellite, the crew conducted experiments including ones on a space station heat pipe radiator, plant division, and crystal growth.

"I'm not a scientist but you do a lot of different jobs up there," Springer said. "I got involved in the science of macro crystallography — growing protein crystals in space. That is the basis of all the pharmaceutical things we have now — process drugs we can't on Earth."

Springer also learned something about himself: he suffered from space sickness.

"Getting sick in space is no fun at all," he admitted. "It did happen to me on my first flight. You know I've got 7,000 hours of flight time. I've been out in the North Atlantic aboard small ships and never got air sick or seasick. Sure enough, on the first flight..."

He said by the second day, he knew he was going to have to use an emesis bag (otherwise known as a barf bag).

"Because of my military background, ... if you get sick in an airplane, the crew chief doesn't clean it up," he explained. "You mess it up, you clean it up."

Not wanting to have to clean things up in no gravity, Springer thought it would be a good idea to firmly hold his emesis bag around his nose and mouth.

"I hurled in the bag," he confessed. "It's zero gravity. It hits the bottom of the bag [and comes right back]. [I was] devastated. My whole life flashed in front of my eyes. I could see the headlines in the newspaper: 'Astronaut dies in his own puke.'"

Thankfully, it got taken care of, and the crew returned to their duties. In addition to their experiments, crew members also would take more than 4,000 photographs of Earth as part of an IMAX project. Springer has a favorite among the photos he took. It depicts the sun setting behind Earth reflecting off the Earth's atmosphere.

"It's 400,000 feet of sensible atmosphere," Springer explained. "I can't imagine anybody flying in space and not coming back an environmentalist. You realize that 400,000 feet of atmosphere is what allows us to live on this planet that we call home." Springer said the first time he saw Earth from space is "forever etched in my memory."

"It was what I expected and more," he beamed during a SC Times interview. "We spent an incredible amount of time looking at the technical aspects of it. From the standpoint of the technology and the science and all of that, it was pretty much what we trained for. The part that you can't really train for is the awe factor of realizing you are circling the globe every nine minutes at a speed of 17,500 mph."

The Discovery mission would touch down on March 18, 1989.

"I no more than got back and the front office called and said we have another flight for you," Springer stated. "That was absolutely delightful."

Springer would next go into space aboard the Atlantis Space Shuttle in 1990. It was the seventh mission dedicated to the U.S. Department of Defense.

"It was a unique mission [to deploy a satellite built by the CIA]," Springer said. He also volunteered to be the medical official on the all-military flight crew. Prior to the launch, he had to learn various medical techniques in case something happened during the flight.

While nothing happened during the mission, prior to launch there were some issues with the vessel. A liquid hydrogen leak was found on the Space Shuttle Columbia, which triggered precautionary tank testing on Atlantis. A hydrogen fuel leak was discovered on an external tank side so Atlantis had to be removed from the launch pad to be fixed. Then there was minor hail damage to the tiles that occurred during a thunderstorm in October. The launch date was then reset to Nov. 9, but had to be reset again to Nov. 15 because of payload problems. The delays turned out to be a blessing in disguise for the U.S. military.

"It was just serendipity," Springer reflected. "The flight [originally] was scheduled for May of 1990. It was delayed until November of that year. As things were progressing in the Middle East (just prior to the Iraqi Conflict).... It turns out we had poor photo imagery of the Middle East. The Department of Defense came to us and asked if we would mind taking pictures of the Middle East as we flew over.... There wasn't one of us who didn't jump to the opportunity. The photos we brought back did provide both the photo intelligence as well as the maps for Operation Desert Storm in 1991."

The Atlantis mission returned to Earth on Nov. 20, 1990. Springer and other crew members would be awarded the Intelligence Achievement Medal for their work taking photos in the Middle East. They were given the awards in a private ceremony and had to keep them hidden. Springer said crews only were allowed to talk about the medals five years after receiving them.

Springer also would leave NASA following the Atlantis mission. He retired from both NASA and the U.S. Marine Corps in December 1990. He had logged more than 237 hours in space.

"I left the program after that second flight," he conceded. "Boeing had come to me and said, 'we want you to be the program manager at the International Space Station for Boeing.'"

It was an opportunity he couldn't pass up.

"I'm very familiar with the space station, but I've never been to it," Springer admitted. "We've had some interesting results and incredible breakthroughs in a variety of areas of science that we do aboard the International Space Station, again primarily in the area of pharmaceutical development."

Springer said the future of space travel will look a lot different going forward.

"We're flying a lot less," he confirmed. "There are only a couple of NASA flights a year."

The shuttle program has been retired, with the space launch system being part of NASA's next vessel.

He added that one of the most interesting things in space now is "the advent of commercial space [ventures] up there."

"There are two dozen companies out there starting their own ventures in space," he stated, adding the public will see commercial space stations up there in the not-too-distant future.

NASA, meanwhile, has started its next phase, Project Artemis, which Springer called "really aggressive." The goal of the project is to enable more lunar exploration and prepare for future missions to Mars. Uncrewed lunar flight tests began in 2022.

While thousands of people have worked to make the space program a success so far, Springer stressed that more people are needed to keep the "spark for discovery" burning bright.
With commercial space travel opening up, he believes there will be more opportunities presented for those bold enough to go after them.

"The youth of today will actually have not only the chance of flying in space but the jobs associated with it in a multitude of fields," he said.

Beyond the Blue: A vivid portrayal of an astronaut's voyage through life, merging the serenity above the blue Earth with the boundless potential of space.

Mary Ellen Weber

*"Mary Ellen Weber shatters the notion that the sky is the limit.
Her journey from Bedford Heights to the cosmos and back,
punctuated by record-breaking skydives and groundbreaking space missions,
illustrates a life lived without boundaries.
As a champion in the sky and a pioneer in space,
Weber's story is a soaring testament to the power of ambition,
proving that with passion and perseverance, one can leap
from the stratosphere of dreams into the orbit of reality."*

The sky isn't the limit for Mary Ellen Weber. Weber isn't only an astronaut — she's also a world record holder. She was part of the world's largest freefall formation with 300 skydivers in 2002. She also holds 19 U.S. National Skydiving Champion medals.

Weber was born Aug. 24, 1962, in Cleveland, though she calls Bedford Heights, Ohio, her hometown. She graduated from Bedford High School in 1980, and four years later earned her Bachelor of Science degree in chemical engineering from Purdue University.

While at Purdue she saw an ad for the Purdue Skydiving Club. The club was basically just someone who would drive people to a dropzone every weekend. She decided to try it out.
In 1983, she started learning with a static line, where there is a cord connecting a skydiver's parachute relay to the plane, so it deploys automatically.

"Actually, skydiving was the first (aspect) of aviation that I got involved with, and it was exhilarating," Weber exclaimed in the book Orbit of Discovery. "It was exciting. It was challenging — very challenging. It's a sport that you can do for many years, and there's always room for improvement and always another challenge around the corner. That's what I liked about both fields, science and aviation."

In 1988, she earned her Ph.D. in physical chemistry from the University of California at Berkeley. Her doctoral research involved the exploration of silicon, particularly the physics of gas-phase chemical reactions. In addition to her work, Weber joined a skydiving team called Deguello. The team is currently the longest-running civilian skydiving team in the United States. In 1989, she became a certified scuba diver as well.

Weber kept extremely busy.

Weber worked for Texas Instruments, where researching new processes for making computer chips led her to work with a group of people from semiconductor companies including SEMATECH and Applied Materials. She helped create a revolutionary reactor for making next-generation computer chips. In 1990, Texas Instruments applied for a patent for one of Weber and Daniel White Jr.'s devices, a uniform gas distributor to a wafer. While she was doing all of that, she also worked to get her pilot's license.

"I was captivated by pure science," Weber remarked during an interview for SkyDiving FanNation, a Sports Illustrated group. "I was at Berkeley for grad school and was enamored by aviation, skydiving, and technology and just decided one day to call up NASA. I thought they would laugh but instead they sent me an application. I never thought I would be selected."

Growing up, there were no female astronauts. It wasn't until three years after she graduated high school that Sally Ride became the first U.S. woman in space. On her first application in 1992, NASA accepted Weber into the astronaut program. She would spend a decade working for NASA. Weber stressed that being an astronaut and skydiving are similar.
"Space is an operational environment," she stated. "It's being able to make decisions and work as a team and follow procedures in critical situations, and there are many operational environments like that .... And certainly skydiving is one of those. Skydiving is about being able to work as a team and do procedures. It's not about analysis when you're in the middle of it. It's about operations."

In addition to her time in space, she worked with technology commercialization — identifying and developing a business venture that leverages space technology. She served on the team that revamped the $2 billion plan for research facilities for the International Space Station. She also was a legislative affairs liaison with NASA's headquarters in Washington, D.C. Her technical assignments included participating in critical launch, landing, and test operations; testing shuttle flight software; and working with international partners to develop training protocols and facilities for experiments aboard the space station.

Weber took her first flight onboard the Discovery Space Shuttle as part of the "all-Ohio" crew.

Unfortunately for Weber, she couldn't skydive while she trained for the mission. NASA regulations forbid any "risky activities" for astronauts assigned to missions. Skydiving is considered such an activity.

During the Discovery mission in July 1995, she was primarily responsible for checking the system of the NASA communications satellite and sending it into its orbit above the equator. Weber also performed biotechnology experiments which included growing colon cancer tissues, which had never happened before. She also served as the medical officer on the flight.

Not skydiving for a bit was worth the experience of seeing Earth from space.

"It is breathtaking. You can see thunderstorms below connected over thousands of miles," Weber recalled during a CBS interview. "As the night passes, that's when the cities pop out like jewels. That's when you can see evidence of humankind."

Orbiting also is a lot different than free falling from 13,000 feet.

"You go all around the world in just 1.5 hours [in space] so you're speeding around the Earth," she explained. "With skydiving, you're pretty much just falling straight down. There's differences not just [with] how high you are, but with the mechanics of the experience itself."

Another difference was space sickness. Unfortunately, on her first flight Weber experienced that on her first day in space. While it took a little bit, she recovered and was able to complete her responsibilities and experiments.

During the mission, Weber also spoke to students in Euclid, Ohio, where she answered questions about what happens when astronauts get sick in space and more.

"The best thing astronauts get to do is fly in space every once in a while. For me one of the best parts of being an astronaut was having the chance to share the experience of space with my friends, my family, and people all over the world," Weber said during a speech at Nile University.

Discovery landed on July 22, 1995. During a post-flight interview, one reporter noted that Weber was the first astronaut born after John Glenn's 1962 mission.

"I'm just proud to be serving in the footsteps of Senator Glenn," she replied.

Weber wasn't on land very long. In 1995, 1997, and 1998, she took part in a twenty-way freefall formation event in the U.S. National Skydiving Championships, receiving silver medals each year. She also took part in the world's largest freefall formation (at that time with 297 people) in 1996.

Weber's second space mission was onboard Atlantis. This was the third shuttle mission devoted to ISS construction. Atlantis launched May 19, 2000, on its ten-day mission, during which crews repaired electrical and life-support components of the station.

Her primary responsibilities included transferring more than 3,000 pounds of equipment from Atlantis to ISS as well as operating the shuttle's robotic arm during spacewalks by fellow astronauts Jeff Williams and Jim Voss. She was responsible for SPACEHAB systems for the cargo carrier housed in the payload bay as well.

Transferring everything through the shuttle to the ISS did cause some clutter, but getting oriented to the station also was an issue.

"Things can be very disorienting," Weber told CNN at the time. "Especially when you come through all these different hatches, when you first enter a new module. It takes you a few seconds to get your bearings and figure out which way is the ceiling and which way is the floor."

Atlantis landed back on Earth on May 29, 2000. The mission was a success, but it had come close to being another disaster. Superheated gasses had breached the shuttle's left wing during re-entry. The Associated Press reported on the issue, calling it "hauntingly similar" to what happened to the Columbia spacecraft.

"There are thousands and thousands of things that can go wrong, and the crew is very much aware this can happen," Weber told the Associated Press. "Certainly, when you learn about this, if it had progressed, it could have been much more dire."

After her second mission to space, Weber went on to receive a Master of Business Administration from Southern Methodist University in 2002. She resigned from NASA in December 2002. During her time with the organization, she earned the NASA Exceptional Service Medal. Though she resigned as an astronaut, she continues to serve on the NASA Advisory Council Committee on Technology, Innovation and Engineering. The committee advises NASA leadership about different technical research and innovations that can benefit any NASA programs.

"I believe that space exploration is extremely important. I believe it is our destiny. I believe it is the future for all humankind. I do believe that one day we will have many space stations, we will have colonies. We will be going to asteroids, planets, and moons," she stressed.

Weber has spoken to several organizations and emphasizes that space exploration is still just beginning.

"The shuttle taught us how to land on the moon and return to the planet, which is the most risky part," she explained when speaking to students. "The space station is helping us in how to live in space for 365 days of the year. We work with things that are far from the Earth. It also teaches us how to go to Mars. It is a very exciting and amazing time. I feel so lucky to have the experience that I have. But I am not going to get the chance to go to the moon or Mars. However, all the young people in this room have."

In addition to her work with space, Weber served for nine years as vice president of UT Southwestern Medical Center, a medical school, research facility, and hospital complex. In 2008, Weber was honored with an Outstanding Chemical Engineer Award from Purdue's School of Chemical Engineering.

Weber also continues to take part in skydiving with the Deguello group. She has completed more than 6,000 skydives to date. In 2023, she took part in a skydiving world record attempt for skydivers over 60.

She founded STELLAR Strategies LLC in 2012. STELLAR is a consulting firm that offers services and strategies for operations "in high-stakes business ventures, technology communications and legislative strategies" to help minimize risk as well as handle emergencies in critical situations.

Weber continues to encourage people to seek opportunities in their life.

"Every time you say no it's to your own detriment because it could be an opportunity to have a brand new experience and change your life," she said. "No matter what age, gender, where you're from, any time an experience presents itself, seriously consider doing it. You don't know what door is going to crack open and present a whole new world to you, spark a passion in you, and lead you down a path you never would've dreamed of or chosen to go down. If you don't at least give it a try, you'll never know."

Legacy of Learning: An homage to the academic roots that underpin the journey of many astronauts, highlighting the connection between education and the exploration of space.

Ronald Sega

*"Ronald Sega's journey from a small town
to the expanse of space is a testament to the transformative
power of education and ambition. His story, starting with a childhood
fascination with Sputnik and culminating in pivotal roles in both the Air Force
and NASA, underscores a life dedicated to exploration and innovation. Sega's
trajectory, shaped by his studies and military discipline, highlights the
extraordinary possibilities that await those who dare to dream
and work towards those dreams with relentless perseverance
and a commitment to lifelong learning."*

Education is vital to opening doors, and the doors it opens can be surprising. For Ohioan Ronald Sega, what was behind those doors was beyond anything he ever could have imagined.

Sega was born Dec. 4, 1952, in Cleveland, though he considers Northfield his hometown.
He graduated from Nordonia High School in Macedonia. In 1974, he earned a Bachelor of Science degree in mathematics and physics from the U.S. Air Force Academy. A year later, Sega earned a Master of Science degree in physics from The Ohio State University. He then earned a doctorate in electrical engineering from the University of Colorado in 1982.

Growing up, Sega knew of the excitement surrounding space exploration. He didn't believe he could become an astronaut but wanted to work hard to contribute in some way to the space program.

"I remember being outside [growing up and] looking at Sputnik, seeing the glint of it sometimes," he recalled during a Denver Post interview. "I also remember being in the third grade sitting on a linoleum floor watching the first launch of Alan Shepard."

Actually going into space didn't seem possible for him.

"I didn't have engineers and scientists that I interacted with," he stated. "I studied hard — math and science were of interest. My first plane ride was from Cleveland to Denver to go to the Air Force Academy. Nobody in my family had been on an airplane before. I didn't think I had a chance of becoming an astronaut. I thought if I worked hard, maybe I could contribute."

After graduating from the U.S. Air Force Academy, Sega was commissioned as a second lieutenant. He completed pilot training in 1976 and then served as an instructor pilot until 1979. From 1979-82, Sega was on the faculty of the U.S. Air Force Academy's Department of Physics. It was there that he designed and constructed a laboratory to investigate microwave fields on the electromagnetic spectrum using infrared techniques.

In 1982, he joined the University of Colorado at Colorado Springs as an assistant professor in the Department of Electrical and Computer Engineering. He was promoted up through the years to professor. Sega served as technical director, lasers and aerospace mechanics directorate, of the Frank J. Seiler Research Laboratory from 1987-88. He also served as research associate professor of physics at the University of Houston, which was affiliated with the Space Vacuum Epitaxy Center for a year. Sega was also the co-principal of the Wake Shield Facility. The facility was a deployable/retrievable experiment platform that was to leave a vacuum wake in low Earth orbit that was to be used to grow deflect-free thin-film layers of gallium arsenide and other semiconductor materials.

The idea to apply for the astronaut program came from individuals Sega had gone to school with in the U.S. Air Force Academy.

"Talking to some of my classmates, actually that were at NASA, they encouraged me to apply," Sega said. "They said 'you have operational experience. You have a research record. You should do it,' and I did. I was very fortunate to have that work out."

Sega applied to the astronaut program and was selected to be an astronaut in 1990. He was selected on his first application to the program. He had several technical assignments with NASA including working on RMS issues for the Astronaut Office Mission Development Branch, supporting orbiter software verification, and serving as the astronaut representative to the Space Station Science and Utilization Advisory Board. He also was chief of astronaut appearances, science support group lead, and part of the space station integration team.

Four years after being accepted as an astronaut, Sega was assigned to his first flight. He was a mission specialist on the 1994 Discovery Space Shuttle. Discovery's mission included the Wake Shield Facility -1 (WSF) and Get Away Special canisters, which would aid radar tracking systems worldwide. SPACEHAB-1 also was launched, involving 12 experiments ranging from life sciences to space dust collection.

Discovery launched on Feb. 3, 1994, on its eight-day mission. The Discovery flight was the first flight of a Russian cosmonaut, Sergei Krikalev, onboard a U.S. space shuttle. It also was the first time a married couple were sent to space together — Sega and his wife at the time, Jan Davis, were both on the mission. The two married in 1990. NASA normally didn't allow couples to be on the same flight, however, Sega and Davis married after being assigned to the mission. Sega was excited about his first journey into space.

"One's first flight in space has its own set of challenges in trying to prepare for a flight in an environment you've never been in," Sega told the Johnson Space Center's Oral History Report. "So I think I was working hard to anticipate anything that could go wrong, and worked hard in that training. ... So the challenge on the first flight was the new environment, service as MS-2 [mission specialist] — kind of flight engineer on ascent and entry as an arm operator — also as the lead on the Wake Shield Facility, which I had worked on prior to joining NASA as a principal investigator and as the program manager prior to joining NASA."

During the mission, Sega's primary responsibilities were the Wake Shield; a sensory joint U.S.-Russian medical investigation; and cabin air, cabin temperature, passive circle and shuttle plume experiment initiation. He also took part in the SAREX amateur radio experiment.

Unfortunately, during Discovery's flight there were several issues with the WSF-1. There was a problem with the satellite's horizon sensor as well as radio interference and glare from the sun.
The WSF-1 was only able to be deployed at the end of the shuttle's Canadarm. It wouldn't be able to be deployed as a free-flying platform until later missions.

Following his initial flight, Sega was made the NASA director of operations at Star City, Russia, from November 1994 to March 1995. He managed NASA activities, such as building an organization and infrastructure to support astronaut and cosmonaut missions and science training for flights to Mir. Sega also was the first American to train in the Russian EVA suit at Star City's hydrolaboratory.

Sega said he found learning the Russian language to be quite difficult.

"By the time of the second space flight, the technical Russian was coming along, but the general conversational and social Russian was very difficult," he said. "Especially if the conversation is not done in context. You'd see a discussion in a particular environment of the Mir station or the simulator about some components or activities, and that would be easier for me to understand and put in context. ... But without context, in a more general conversation with colloquial expressions, it was more difficult."

Sega praised the Russians who were part of his office for their help. He also said he learned a lot about the different kinds of preparation Russia did for their missions as opposed to a space shuttle flight.

"In many ways there are similarities of crew training, but in many ways that's different," Sega pointed out. "The Russian training system certainly has differences from ours, and the equipment and other support structure for our side of the activity was also more difficult to put all of the parts in place because of the distance involved in obtaining spare parts and those types of things."

In 1996, Sega would return to space as part of the Space Shuttle Atlantis Crew. The flight was the third docking mission with the Russian Space Station Mir and included the transfer of astronaut Shannon Lucid to Mir. Lucid would be the first American woman to live on Mir and the beginning of a continuous U.S. presence in space that lasted years.

Atlantis launched March 22, 1996, on its nine-day mission. The launch had been delayed once due to concerns about winds. Sega served as the payload commander and a mission specialist. His primary responsibilities included SPACEHAB, Biorack, and more. He again spoke to students on the ham radio during the mission.

Sega also was responsible for planning and on-orbit operations including the transfer of 4,800 pounds of science and mission hardware, food, water, and air to Mir. The crew also had to return more than 1,100 pounds of science and hardware to Earth.

Atlantis landed on March 31, 1996. Later that year, Sega would retire from NASA. During his time with the organization, Sega earned two NASA Space Flight Medals and a Superior Achievement Medal. Later he earned the NASA Outstanding Leadership Medal in 1997.

After leaving NASA, Sega became dean of engineering and applied sciences at the University of Colorado, a position he held until 2001. Sega said he saw a lot of potential in his students and gave advice to those who wish to be astronauts.

"The space program needs are varied," he pointed out when speaking to the Johnson Space Center Oral History Project. "In our college, we span hardware and software kinds of disciplines. So I will talk to the students, encourage them to continue their studies and do as well as they possibly can, whatever they choose, but there are a variety of roles that they can fill in being involved in the space program. There are some that involve flying in space. Many involve support of those operations in space. Many more involve the design, test and building of equipment that will be involved in the program, as well as some of the scientific underpinnings, ground-based, as well as spaced-based work, for the program."

After leaving NASA, Sega continued his extensive career in government service as well as academia and the private sector. He retired from the U.S Air Force in 2005 as a major general. Sega served as the director of defense research and engineering for the Office of the Secretary of Defense, reserve assistant to the Chief of the Air Force Reserve, and reserve assistant to the chairman of the Joint Chiefs of Staff at the Pentagon after leaving NASA.

In 2005, Sega became the Under Secretary of the Air Force — serving as the U.S. Department of Defense's executive agent and milestone decision authority for space. In that capacity, Sega "developed, coordinated and integrated plans and programs for space systems and the acquisition of all DoD [Department of Defense] space major defense acquisition programs," according to the American Institute of Aeronautics and Astronautics.

In addition, Sega helped facilitate a U.S. space industrial base study and an international space partnership with Australia. He went on to be chief technical officer of the U.S. Army Futures Demand. He also acted as vice president and enterprise executive for energy and the environment at both Colorado State University and The Ohio State University.
Sega has several earned additional honors. He has been the recipient of the Air Force Meritorious Service Medal, Commendation Medal, Reserve Achievement Medal, and Air Force Research Fellow — Air Force Office of Scientific Research.

He also has authored or co-authored 150 technical publications. In 2012, Sega — acting as vice chair of the National Research Council's Committee on NASA's Strategic Direction — testified before Congress about NASA's strategic direction and space policy.

"NASA has been tugged in multiple directions the past several years," he stated. "Despite a turbulent policy environment, the agency has made many astonishing accomplishments. There remains, however, a lack of consensus on the agency's future direction among the United States' political leadership."
Sega went on to state that "without such a consensus the agency cannot be expected to develop or work effectively toward long-term priorities."

He stressed there was a mismatch between the budget allocated to NASA by Congress and NASA's priorities. He said while NASA develops a strategic plan, its goals are set by the national leadership, which is mixed most times on what should be pursued. He outlined several options including: a restructuring program for NASA; engaging in and committing to long-term, cost-sharing partnerships including with international partners and private industries; increasing the size of NASA budget; and reducing the size of NASA program portfolio (human exploration, Earth and space sciences, aeronautics, and space technology) in favor of the other elements.

The committee recommended NASA work with other government agencies to efficiently coordinate the nation's aeronautics and space activities while leading a more international approach to space efforts. Sega also praised NASA's civil service and contractor staff for their superb work. He also noted their frustration over the limitations imposed on NASA by a lack of consensus on the organization's long-term direction.

"Only with the national consensus on the agency's future direction ... can NASA continue to deliver the wonder, the knowledge, the national security and economy benefits, and the technology that typifies its history," Sega stated.

Despite Sega's plea, a national consensus on NASA's strategic plans was never set up. However, the organization did decide to increase its partnerships with other governments and public agencies going forward. Projects with partners that are on the horizon include the Artemis program, which plans to return to the moon; the Dragonfly rotorcraft that will explore sites on Saturn's moon, Titan; a reconnaissance mission of Jupiter's moon, Europa; and more. The next generation of astronauts, engineers, and scientists will need to undertake these projects.

During a commencement at Pueblo Community College in 2016, Sega stressed the need for continued education, not just for the space program but for anything in the future.

"The importance of education is clearly there," Sega said. "We're in the 21st century, which is characterized by an increasing rate of change of technology, of complexity. They need to continue to learn and continue to improve. They'll open a lot of options, a lot of doors for them going forward, which is important."

United in Exploration: His collaborative efforts required by all in space travel, showcase his camaraderie and shared purpose among his fellow astronauts.

Ronald Parise

*"Ronald Parise's story is one of celestial dreams
turned reality, a testament to the power of persistent curiosity and
the pursuit of knowledge. From his Ohio roots to the vastness of space,
Parise's journey was fueled by a lifelong fascination with the stars and the
mysteries they hold. His legacy, etched in the annals of space exploration,
serves as a beacon, guiding future generations to look up at the night sky
not just with wonder, but with the ambition to explore
and understand the infinite universe."*

Curiosity coupled with the goal of aiming for the stars can get a person very far. Ever since Ronald Parise was little, he would look up at the stars with wonder.

"I have always been interested in spaceflight and astronomy," Parise stated in a NASA Teacher's Guide publication. "As a child, I followed the early space program closely; I read books on the stars and planets. Astronomy was fascinating to me because of the questions it brought to mind: 'does the universe go on forever?' 'If it doesn't go forever what's on the other side of it?' "

Those were questions Parise hoped to answer. As a teenager, he was involved in an amateur astronomy group — the Mahoning Valley Astronomical Society — and even made his own astronomical observations.

"Another interesting thing is that astronomy is not an experimental science like physics, chemistry or biology, in which you can perform an experiment to prove a theory," he reflected. "You can't do that because the astronomical objects are at such vast distances. We have to be content with observing the electromagnetic radiation that they emit."
The challenge is to develop new ways to observe that radiation. It was a challenge Parise accepted. The first stop was to learn what he could about the stars and the rest of the universe.

He graduated from Western Reserve High School in 1969, then went on to receive a Bachelor of Science degree in physics from Youngstown State University in 1973. He would earn his Master of Science degree and Doctor of Philosophy degree in astronomy from the University of Florida in 1977 and 1979, respectively. Parise had hoped to be an astronaut for several years.

In the late 1970s, he applied twice to be a NASA specialist. He even applied in graduate school — one of 8,700 applicants.

"I didn't even get an interview," he stated.

Parise went on to work for Operations Research Inc., which developed avionic requirements and performed analysis for NASA missions at Goddard Space Flight Center, then for the Computer Sciences Corporation, which had a number of contacts with NASA. He went on to be part of a team that would design and build electric controls for telescopes, many of which would be part of NASA payloads.

NASA then sent word out in 1983 that they were looking for more mission specialists, specifically scientists. Parise applied again. In 1984, NASA selected three astronomers to train as astronauts for shuttle missions scheduled for 1986 and 1987, and Parise was among them. The trio were selected for their extensive backgrounds in space science.

Parise had some experience flying as well, possessing a private pilot's license. He also was interested in amateur radio, something he would use on his space missions. Originally, Parise had been slated to go into space in March 1986 in the Astro-1 Spacelab mission. The mission was to take astronomical observations of Halley's Comet. Parise and another astronaut-astronomer Sam Durrance had been training for that mission when a national tragedy put that plan on hold. After the Challenger disaster, payload specialists did not fly again until 1990.

The Astro-1 Spacelab would fly in 1990, though it could not observe Halley's comet like originally planned. The objectives for the mission instead had been changed to around-the-clock observations of the celestial sphere. Parise and Durrance would travel onboard the Space Shuttle Columbia on an eight-day mission. The shuttle lifted off on Dec. 2, 1990, after several delays. It had been first scheduled on May 16, 1990, however there were several issues that forced the launch to be bumped back several months, including a faulty freon coolant loop valve, a leakage in an umbilical, and a malfunction in part of the payload.

The Astro-1 lab would have four telescopes — the Hopkins Ultraviolet Telescope, Wisconsin Ultraviolet Photo-Polarimeter Experiment, the Ultraviolet Imaging Telescope (UIT), and the Broad Band X-Ray Telescope. Parise was excited about the mission and what could be learned from it. He praised astronomy as a "very fundamental science."

"Man has always been interested in what his world was all about, how it got here, where it came from, what's going to happen to it, what the whole structure of this thing we live in is," he observed during a United Press International interview in 1990. "We can't just stop working on it. We don't spend a whole lot of money working on it. It may seem that way sometimes, but in the overall scheme of things it's really a very small amount of money and a small amount of effort that we put into trying to answer some of these really fundamental questions."

During the mission scientists would use the telescopes to study X-ray and ultraviolet radiation from deep space. Parise was intimately familiar with one of the telescopes. He had helped develop the UIT's electronic system as well as flight hardware.

Scientists encountered numerous technical glitches during the mission. According to NASA, the "data volume was less than half of that originally planned" and only about 67 percent of the stated goals were completed. Still, when Astro-1 returned to Earth on Dec. 11, it had made 231 observations of 130 unique astronomical targets. The UIT alone had captured images including reflection nebulae, supernova remnants, spiral and dwarf galaxies, and more.

The mission also had an amateur radio experiment, which Parise operated — becoming the first ham operator to radio from space. Parise operated the amateur radio system, called SAREX (Shuttle Amateur Radio Experiment), during periods when he wasn't scheduled for orbiter or other payload activities. This meant that whenever the shuttle was above the Earth and Parise was on it, amateur ham stations and operators could communicate with the space shuttle. Using the amateur ratio, Parise was able to communicate with amateur radio operators, school children, and others during the flight. Parise had hoped to contact Mir through the ham radio but wasn't able to because of timing problems and interference. Parise still loved the adventure.

"To leave our home world and look back at it from space is the most incredible experience," he would state.

While Parise had fun on the flight, he did experience some difficulties. Speaking at Goddard Space Flight Center after his return, one child had asked what astronauts do after landing.

"You sit there and try to stand up," he answered earnestly. "You get unstrapped and find you can't stand up. It takes a while to be able to put weight on your legs again. You find out once you stand up, you can't keep your balance. You feel like you're going to fall down."

Parise also stated he lost about ten pounds while in space — all of it water.

"You pee a lot," he admitted. "There's always a line in the bathroom the first day or two in space."

Parise's second flight was onboard the Space Shuttle Endeavour in 1995. Endeavour would take the Astro-2 lab into space. The goal of the mission was to observe and explore remotely the universe using ultraviolet wavelengths of light. Endeavour launched on May 2, 1995, and landed more than sixteen days later, making it one of the longest space flights yet. It also hit one other milestone — it was the first advertised shuttle mission connected to the Internet. Crews would answer some of the 2.4 million requests they received from more than 200,000 Internet users across 59 counties.

The more than two-week mission had a very astronomy-driven focus, however one of the three telescopes, which were to automatically lock on targets, malfunctioned.

"Boy, the [pointing system] is driving all over the place," Parise grumbled during the flight. He and Durrance had to manually point the telescope.

Astro-2 detected intergalactic helium, which confirmed one of the major predictions about the Big Bang theory. Observations from the lab would add to scientists' understanding of the origins of stars and the history of the universe, something Parise had worked to discover since his youth. Parise's personal contributions to the two Astro missions provided scientists with "an unprecedented view of our universe, expanding our understanding of the birth, life and death of stars and galaxies," according to Frank Bauer, chairman of the Amateur Radio on the International Space Station.

Parise also took his ham radio back into space. According to NASA, Parise and other crew members took "on the role of teachers as they educated students in the United States and other countries about their mission objectives" using the SAREX II. The ham radio portion of the mission would be one of Parise's prime responsibilities, along with Astro-2. He later would be credited with creating the amateur radio presence on the International Space Station, which allows students to speak with astronauts and learn about space.

U.S. Rep. Tim Ryan would later say, "Dr. Parise established the radio communications link that inspired countless students to study and seek careers in vitally important scientific fields. This radio connection brought about the interest and devotion to outer space that we see today."

After his final flight, Parise took on a support role in advanced planning and communications engineering for a variety of space mission projects including Mir and the International Space Station. He also took part in several astronomical research projects for Earth-based observatories. His work on circumstellar matter in binary star systems and the evolutionary status of stars in globular clusters was published.

Parise was an astronaut for 12 years but continued to support NASA for many more. He worked on advanced communication planning for space missions through the Goddard Space Flight Center and the Networks and Mission Services Project. He also was involved in the Advanced Architectures and Automation Branch to help develop standard Internet protocols in space data transmission systems.

During his time at NASA, he earned several honors including: two NASA Space Flight Medals, the NASA/Goddard Space and Flight Center Special Act Award and Community Service Award, and several NASA Group Achievement Awards. He also was honored with the Computer Sciences Corp Award for Technical Innovation and the Allied Signal Quest for Excellence Award. In 1996, he received an honorary Doctor of Science degree from Youngstown State University.

During his time as a mission specialist, Parise continued to work at Computer Sciences Corporation. After leaving NASA, Parise also enjoyed going to schools as a motivational speaker to inspire students to pursue science degrees.

Parise died in 2008 of brain cancer. He was 56. Upon his passing, individuals were asked to donate to Youngstown State University Foundation's Dr. Ronald A. Parise Scholarship Fund. The fund aids students looking to pursue technical degrees. Congressman Ryan on March 3, 2009, gave a tribute to Parise in the U.S. House of Representatives.

"Dr. Ronald Anthony Parise touched countless lives through his contributions to his community, his nation and the world of science and for this he will never be forgotten," Ryan stated.

In 2016, a historical marker was erected in Warren to honor Parise. During the dedication ceremony, Parise was praised as "one of Warren's most acclaimed and brilliant sons." The marker is located near the entrance to the Apollo 11 Neil Armstrong First Flight Memorial and near Parise's childhood home. Bauer said that Parise's legacy continues to grow.

"Ron Parise was — and continues to be — an inspiration to countless students, ham radio operators and friends all over the world," Bauer said in a statement. "His accomplishments were many, including space explorer, pioneer, astrophysicist, pilot, ham radio operator, avionics and software expert, inspirational speaker and motivator, student satellite mentor, husband, father and friend."

Homage to Heritage: An astronaut's reflection on the ties to home and the pride of representing one's roots on the global stage of space.

Gregory Harbaugh

*"Gregory Harbaugh's odyssey from a starry-eyed boy in Ohio
to a seasoned astronaut illustrates a profound dedication to reaching the
cosmos. His journey, marked by persistence, intelligence,
and a passion for space exploration, demonstrates
that with unwavering focus and hard work,
even the loftiest dreams can be grounded in reality.
Harbaugh's story is a vivid reminder that for those who dare
to look skyward and tirelessly pursue their ambitions,
the vastness of space is not just a destination
but a realm of endless possibilities."*

While being an astronaut is a dream for some people, for others it is their "life ambition." Gregory Harbaugh was determined that one day he would walk among the stars, and he worked to achieve his goal.

Harbaugh was born April 15, 1956, in Cleveland. He grew up in Willoughby, Ohio, graduating from Willoughby South High School in 1974. He went on to earn a Bachelor of Science degree in aeronautical and astronautical engineering from Purdue University in 1978. He later received a Master of Science degree in physical science from the University of Houston-Clear Lake in 1986. In addition to his schooling, Harbaugh would earn his commercial pilot's license with instrument rating.

Between earning his bachelor's and master's degree, Harbaugh went to work at NASA's Johnson Space Center. He worked in space shuttle flight operations, working from Mission Control starting with the first orbital flight of the space shuttle program in 1981. He also supported flight operations from Mission Control during his time as an astronaut. Harbaugh was a lead data processing systems officer for several flights.

Working at NASA, Harbaugh heard right away when the organization was looking for more astronauts and made sure his application was submitted. He was determined to be an astronaut. In June 1987, Harbaugh was one of 15 people selected as an astronaut out of 2,000 applicants.

"I wasn't the smartest guy. I didn't have the best resume, but I was determined to see this through," Harbaugh said, speaking to students at Lemon Bay High School in 2002.

Harbaugh had several technical assignments before he reached space. During his time at NASA as an astronaut, he worked in the Shuttle Avionics Integration Laboratory and with the Shuttle Remote Manipulator system, telerobotics systems development for the space station, EVA activities, and more. Four years after becoming an astronaut and going through training, Harbaugh went on his first flight. He was very excited for the opportunity.

"I don't think you ever get jaded about the excitement of a launch," Harbaugh exclaimed during a 1991 UPI interview. He added that being an astronaut on the flight would give him a whole new vantage point on a launch. "From an anticipation standpoint, I don't have much of a chance to sit around and think about what lies ahead. But I will say, every now and then in the simulators, it sort of hits you that you're going to be doing all of this from space. You can't help but say 'gee whiz, I can't wait to do that.'"

Harbaugh's first flight was as part of the Space Shuttle Discovery's crew. Discovery's mission was dedicated to the U.S. Department of Defense. Among the payload was an infrared background signature survey, radiation monitoring equipment, and other experiments. During the flight, the crew gathered information about rocket plumes against the Earth and into the darkness of space in order to develop heat sensitive infrared sensors to distinguish different missiles in flight.

"Anything we can do to research the capabilities that we think we might need to defend ourselves as a country is a smart thing to do," Harbaugh stated about the mission's goals.

Discovery was originally scheduled to launch on March 9, 1991, however cracks were found on lug hinges on the external tank mechanisms. The launch was rescheduled for April 23, but was again postponed after out-of-specification readings. Discovery then launched on April 28, 1991, for its eight-day mission. Harbaugh talked about his first flight during Cedar Point's Physics Day in 1993.

"It is the deepest, darkest black you can imagine," he reflected about space. "There's nothing like being in the cabin of the shuttle, looking out into space and feeling the depth of the universe."

Besides the Department of Defense payloads, the shuttle crew also marked the 30th anniversary of astronaut Alan Shepard becoming the first American in space.

Harbaugh worked with the remote manipulator system robot arm and was responsible for the infrared background signature survey spacecraft during the mission. After his flight, he was awarded an Aviation Week and Space Technology Laurel, one of two laurels he would earn from the organization.

Harbaugh returned to space in 1993 on board the Space Shuttle Endeavour. The nearly six-day mission was to deploy a tracking and data relay satellite. Crews also had experiments that collected x-ray radiation data from sources in deep space and experiments to test microgravity, study plant growth, examine how human bones adapt to space, and more.

Harbaugh also took part in his first spacewalk — spending nearly five hours with astronaut Mario Runco as they conducted tasks to help increase NASA's knowledge of how people could work in space in preparation for the construction of a space station.

"We are trying to help identify outer boundaries of the human performance envelope, if you will, in doing spacewalks," Harbaugh stated.

During the flight, astronauts took questions from elementary school students at their alma maters. The session was called "Physics of Toys," with crew members using toys to describe physics in space to the students. Harbaugh answered questions from students at Thomas A. Edison Elementary School in Willoughby while conducting experiments with a basketball and magnetic marbles.

The third time Harbaugh went to space was on board the Space Shuttle Atlantis for the first shuttle-Mir space station docking. The shuttle dropped off equipment as well as cosmonauts Anatoly Solovyev and Nikolai Budarin. It also picked up astronaut Norman Thagard from Mir.
The nine-day mission originally was set for May 1995, but was moved back so the Russian space program could reconfigure station docking and conduct procedures to prepare for the space station to dock. Weather caused the mission to be delayed on June 23 and 24, 1995. Atlantis would launch June 27.

Harbaugh had several prime responsibilities during the mission including the orbiter docking mechanism, lasers, EVA, in-flight maintenance, photography, and earth observations. Harbaugh enjoyed being on Mir.

"I feel like we're visiting a Russian dacha," Harbaugh quipped to Mission Control. "It very much is home over here to these folks, and to be welcomed as we have been with really open arms has been a great pleasure."

After undocking from Mir, Atlantis flew around the space station taking pictures to assess its condition. Afterwards, Harbaugh praised the team effort it took to make the first Mir-Shuttle docking a success.

Harbaugh's fourth flight was onboard Discovery. The six-member crew served and upgraded the Hubble Space Telescope. The nearly ten-day mission launched on Feb. 11, 1997. Harbaugh and fellow astronaut Joe Tanner would replace a degraded fine guidance sensor and failed engineering and science tape recorder. They also installed an optical control electronics enhancement kit. While the two were out doing repairs on Feb 14, 1997, they noticed cracking and wearing on the thermal insulation on the side of the Hubble.

Two days later the duo replaced a solar array device electronics package and fitted insulated blankets over the rips in the Teflon cover of the Hubble Space Telescope they had seen earlier.

"I think we can declare victory on this one," he said of the work while outside the shuttle. He then turned back to look at Earth. After several flights, the view still awed him. "Look at that planet up there," he reflected. "Unbelievable."

After his fourth flight, Harbaugh remained with NASA. In 1997, Harbaugh was the acting manager of NASA's spacewalk projects office. During the last four years he was with the agency, he was director of its EVA program. With that program, he oversaw the development of spacewalk techniques and requirements. He also helped oversee spacewalk requirements for the assembly and operation of the International Space Station.

During his time with the organization, he was the recipient of the NASA Distinguished Service Medal, Exceptional Service Medal, Exceptional Achievement Medal and four Space Flight Medals. In 1999, he was awarded the Rotary National Award for Space Achievement "Stellar Award" for outstanding leadership. He also earned the John Hopkins Presidential Medal and the Sigma Chi Fraternity Significant Sig Award. Harbaugh also was awarded a Purdue University Outstanding Aerospace Engineer and Astronaut Alumnus Award.

Harbaugh left NASA in 2001. While being an astronaut was his ambition, it was love for his family that led him to leave space behind.

"Every time before I left [on a mission], I'd write them a letter saying goodbye. That letter got harder and harder to write. I became more and more aware of things that might go wrong," he stated when talking to students in 2002.

Though he left NASA, Harbaugh continued to advocate for the need for space travel. Following the Space Shuttle Columbia's disintegration upon re-entry to Earth in 2003, Harbaugh spoke to reporters stating that NASA officials would find the cause (which was insulating foam from the shuttle's external tank striking the tiles on the orbiter's wind during lift off. The damage allowed atmospheric gas to go past the heat shield, which destroyed the shuttle's left wing upon re-entry).

"It sickens me to see this kind of loss," Harbaugh said of the death of the seven astronauts onboard. "But it is a reminder that we put people into an environment that is dangerous to humans.

"The question in my mind is where we go from here. We have several ideas and proposals for the next generation vehicle and we need to get started. But the real question is: What do we want to accomplish with our space program?"

The Columbia disaster happened during construction of the International Space Station, which was put on hold for more than two years following Columbia's loss. Harbaugh stressed that NASA and the nation really needed to focus on what their goal was for space.

"Do we want to explore nearby?" he asked. "Do we want commercial dividends? Or do we want to expand farther out? ... And it doesn't make sense that we went to the moon and then forgot about it. From the pure human species' natural instinct, we have to go to Mars. Right now, there is no national will."

Harbaugh pointed out that the knowledge from the Hubble Space Telescope alone has changed the field of astronomy. He stressed there is so much more to learn from space and that the future needs to have eyes on the stars.

"The laws of physics are still not fully known to us. We must continue asking questions [through space exploration]," he said. "Who knows? Maybe one day we will have the holodeck and transporter." He stressed that the nation and world need to keep aiming for the stars. "If you do not set the sights above the horizon, people quit looking up," Harbaugh warned.

Harmony in the Heavens: A symphony of science and music, capturing the astronaut's multifaceted contributions to exploration and culture.

Carl Walz

*"Carl Walz's journey from the streets of Cleveland
to the International Space Station epitomizes a life driven by
a relentless pursuit of the stars. An astronaut and musician, Walz's
career harmonizes the precision of science with the creativity of art,
proving that the realms of space exploration and personal passions
can coexist. His story, from piloting spacecraft to strumming chords
in zero gravity, is a vivid illustration of how dedication, talent,
and a sense of adventure can elevate one's dreams from
mere aspirations to extraordinary realities."*

Astronauts may seem like rockstars to many, but some sort of are. Carl Walz was not only an astronaut, he was also the lead singer of a rock-n-roll band made entirely of astronauts called Max Q. Walz even managed to get a keyboard for himself to play while he was stationed on the International Space Station (ISS).

He was born Sept. 6, 1955, in Cleveland. Walz had wanted to be an astronaut since he was a kid, he told the Kent Stater Newspaper in 1991. Walz graduated from Charles F. Brush High School in Lyndhurst in 1973 and went on to earn a Bachelor of Science degree in physics from Kent State University in 1977. In 1979, he was awarded a Master of Science degree in solid state physics from John Carroll University.

While he was at Kent State, Walz was part of the Air Force Reserve Officers Training Corps (AFROTC). He then was commissioned as a second lieutenant in the U.S. Air Force. Walz has praised his education and the AFROTC for helping him become an astronaut.

"My major in physics definitely helped, and the Air Force ROTC helped me to learn a lot about airplanes and the space program," he confirmed. "I don't think I'd be where I am today without the AFROTC."

While with the Air Force, Walz became responsible for analysis of radioactive samples. The samples were from the 1155th Technical Operations Squadron's Atomic Energy Detection System in California.

"I had met people — at that first assignment [with the nuclear research lab] — who had applied to become astronauts in the 1978 astronaut class," Walz said, speaking at the John Carroll Alumni Continuing Education Series. "I talked to those guys and they kind of set me on my path to become an astronaut. They recommended going to the Air Force Test Pilot School. Now at the time I wasn't a test pilot, but they had a parallel course as a light test engineer, so I signed up for that."

The Air Force selected him to take part as a flight test engineer at test pilot school in 1983. From 1984-87, Walz was the flight test engineer to the F-16 Combined Test Force at Edwards Air Force Base. In that capacity, Walz worked on a variety of F-16C avionics and armament development programs. He then became the flight test manager at the Air Force Flight Test Center from 1987-90.

As soon as he got out of test pilot school, Walz began applying to be an astronaut.

"I applied four times," Walz stated. "I just had to keep applying each time and each time I got a little bit closer."

Walz finally was accepted into the astronaut program in 1990.

"I was assigned in fairly fast order to three space shuttle flights in 1993, 1994, and 1996," Walz commented. "Each one of those a slightly different kind of flight and then I was assigned to the space station program."

Before he could go to space, he had to undergo his astronaut training. He also joined a band.
During his time at NASA, Walz became part of the group Max Q. Walz was on vocals, though he also could play the keyboard. He had been a church accompanist in high school and also played and sang in the Fabulous Blue Moons while in Cleveland.

Walz made his first space flight as a member of the Space Shuttle Discovery's crew in 1993.
The goal of the nearly ten-day mission was to deploy the U.S. Advanced Communications Technology Satellite, Shuttle Pallet Satellite, and conduct research experiments.

Discovery was to launch on July 17, 1993, but was canceled due to a premature charging of solid rocket boosters hold down bolts and a liquid hydrogen vent arm. The launch was delayed three more times for a variety of technical issues. Discovery finally launched on Sept. 12, 1993.

Walz had several responsibilities on the flight including the Advanced Communications Technology Satellite, performing tasks to evaluate spacewalkers' mobility, evaluating tools, taking photos, in-flight maintenance, and more. During the mission, Walz took part in a seven-hour spacewalk to evaluate tools for an upcoming Hubble Space Telescope servicing mission.

"Boy is that beautiful down there," Walz said in awe as the shuttle flew over the Atlantic Ocean during his spacewalk.

"We can see the entire world," Walz told UPI while onboard. "It gives you a new feeling of how we need to take care of our environment to preserve it for our grandchildren."

Speaking of family, Walz made sure to scribble a note — holding it out to the camera to wish his wife a happy 17th wedding anniversary during the flight.

Discovery landed back on Earth on Sept. 22, 1993. Walz returned to space the following year on Columbia. His second flight would set a new flight duration record for the shuttle program.
Walz was assigned as a crew member to Columbia for NASA's second International Microgravity Laboratory spacelab module. The 15-day mission would have more than 80 experiments onboard to research material and life sciences.

Columbia launched on July 8, 1994, for its mission. Once again, Walz oversaw in-flight maintenance and took photos during the mission. He also was responsible for the Military Application of Ship Tracks (MAST) and aided with the performance assessment workstation and numerous experiments including those on white blood cells and space-induced calcium loss.

While Walz was in space, Max Q had a gig. The band played at a celebration of the 25th anniversary of Apollo 11, where they opened for Cheap Trick. Walz was in orbit so he couldn't be there that night. He was there in spirit, however, as his official NASA portrait was on the mike stand.

In orbit, Walz also celebrated Apollo 11. The crew gathered for a live telecast to commemorate the event. Columbia made landfall on July 23, 1994, after making 236 orbits around the Earth, setting a new flight-duration record.

The third time Walz went into space was onboard Atlantis in 1996. The shuttle docked with the Russian Mir station to deliver food, water, scientific experiments, equipment, and to exchange NASA long-duration members. The flight brought back Shannon Lucid, who spent 188 days in space setting the world record for a woman and a new U.S. spaceflight record.

Atlantis' mission was ten days long. It launched Sept. 16, 1996, after delays because of switching boosters and weather issues. Atlantis docked with the Mir on Sept. 18, with hatches opening a day later. During the five days Atlantis was docked, crews would transfer more than 4,000 pounds of supplies to the space station as well as experiments.

Walz's responsibilities included the orbiter docking system, EVA, real-time radiation monitoring, extreme temperature translation furnace, the orbiter space vision system, Mir photo survey, video, and more.

Walz also talked to students at Immaculate Conception School in Celina, Ohio, as well as students in Andover, Kan. and Surrey, England, using the amateur radio equipment. One student asked if his bones got sore or if he felt different because of the weightlessness.

"My back is a little sore from being weightless, but that's part of your body getting adjusted to not having gravity," he answered. "Over time, it gets better and you feel great."

Atlantis landed on September 26, 1996. Walz had been on the Russian Space Station, but his next flight would take him to the International Space Station (ISS). Walz's fourth mission was his most challenging yet. He spent years preparing for it. In 2001, Walz had to give up his role in Max Q when he was assigned Expedition 4. Expedition 4 was the fourth resident crew expedition to ISS.

In 2001, Walz as well as fellow astronaut Daniel Bursch and cosmonaut Yuri Onufrienko embarked from the Space Shuttle Endeavour for ISS. The trio were scheduled to be in space for several months. In his personal effects, Walz had taken with him a sweatshirt and medallion that he later presented to Kent State University President Carol Cartwright. Also on the flight was an electric keyboard, which Walz used during his time at ISS.

On Dec. 5, 2001, Endeavour launched. Two days later, Walz, Bursch and Onufrienko became the official residents of the ISS. The trio were to help ISS expand its science investigations. While Endeavour was still docked and the Expedition 3 crew was onboard ISS, Walz and Expedition 3 member Mikhail Tyurin played an impromptu concert for the crews.

"The strangest thing about playing music in space is that it's not strange," Walz pointed out, adding that many homes have musical instruments. He later added, "I think it's fitting that in a home in space you have musical instruments as well. It's natural. Music makes it seem less like a spaceship and more like a home."

Endeavour undocked from ISS, taking with it the Expedition 3 crew and leaving the Expedition 4 crew behind on Dec. 15, 2001. Besides the experiments, the Expedition 4 crew also had to conduct several spacewalks for various reasons and do maintenance tasks. On Jan. 14, 2002, Walz and Onufrienko did a spacewalk to relocate a cargo boom as well as install a radio antenna. In February, Walz and Bursch tested the Quest Airlock to prepare it for four upcoming spacewalks for another shuttle crew. Walz wore both U.S. and Russian spacesuits during his walks.

The Expedition 4 crew stayed longer than what was intended on ISS. The three were only to remain in orbit until May 2002. The trip was extended so Endeavour's visiting astronauts could fix the station's robotic arm, then there needed to be a wrist-joint replacement that required an extra month. When Endeavour arrived during Walz's stay on June 8, 2002, the commander was Ken Cockrell, Max Q's keyboard player.

"So we made sure we found time to play a song — me on guitar, him on keyboards," said Walz. "It was Van Morrison's 'Brown-Eyed Girl,' and we used the Leonardo module as our studio."

Though they were getting ready to go, days before they were set to leave ISS something happened that must have made Walz and others wonder if they would be staying even longer.
On June 8, 2002, Carl radioed down to Mission Control after he heard an unusual noise outside of the Unity module.

"We're hearing a pretty loud, audible noise, kind of a growling noise, from inside the node," he stated.

One of the control movement gyroscopes, which control the station's orientation, had a mechanical failure. The station could run with the three operational ones and did so until the malfunctioning one was repaired in 2005.

On June 11, 2002, Bursch and Walz broke NASA's space endurance record at that time of 188 days. The Expedition 4 crew left the ISS on June 15 onboard Endeavour. They would get home June 19, 2002, having spent 194 days in orbit.

Upon his return from ISS, Walz served as the director of Advanced Capabilities Division in the Exploration Systems Mission Directorate at NASA. It was a position he held until his retirement. In that office, Walz was responsible for items such as lunar robotics exploration, nuclear power, human research and technology development. Walz retired from the U.S. Air Force after 24 years of service in 2003. In December 2008, he decided to retire as an astronaut as well and go into the private sector.

"NASA owes a great debt to Carl Walz for his service as an astronaut and the expertise and perspective he has shared with us in the Advanced Capabilities Division," said Doug Cooke, associate administrator for the Exploration Systems Mission Directorate at NASA, of Walz's retirement. "The legacy of his leadership will be strongly felt in the next generation of manned space missions."

His work in the private sector still features space and space explorers heavily. In 2009, Walz became vice president for human space flight operations for Orbital Sciences Corp.'s Advanced Programs Group. He was responsible for mission operations for Orbital regarding research and development with NASA as well as commercial resupply services missions with the International Space Station.

Walz then became the director of business development for Oceaneering and in 2022, the business development consultant for Oceaneering Space Systems (OSS). In 2022, OSS and Collins Aerospace teams were selected to develop the next-generation extravehicular spacesuits for NASA.

"These suits will provide a better fit and comfort for the astronauts, increasing their mobility to safely operate on the surface of the moon," Walz commented in a press release.

Reflections on the Orbital Plane: Celebrating the achievements in an all-Ohio space shuttle mission and the personal milestones of the astronauts who paved the way.

Donald Thomas

"Donald Thomas' journey from a young boy in Cleveland, dreaming under a starlit sky, to an accomplished astronaut is a testament to unwavering determination and passionate pursuit of one's dreams. His story, marked by perseverance through repeated rejections and relentless self-improvement, is a powerful reminder that the road to achieving extraordinary goals is often paved with resilience and hard work. Thomas' dedication to bringing a piece of Ohio with him to space and his commitment to research and education echo a profound message: No dream is too distant, and no effort is too great, in the quest to reach the stars."

No one can say Donald Thomas doesn't do his research. He also has a real "taste" for Ohio.

Donald A. Thomas was born May 6, 1955, in Cleveland. Thomas knew he wanted to be an astronaut since he was six. He even remembers the date — May 6, 1961, when Alan Shepard became the first man in the United States to enter space on board his Freedom 7 Mercury capsule.

"At that time, I was in elementary school, and I remember how they gathered all the students to the floor of the school's gymnasium to watch the momentous feat on a small black and white television," he recalled during an interview for Parent Circle magazine. "I remember sitting there and saying 'I want to do that.' ... I wanted to ride a rocket to space. I wanted to experience zero gravity out there, and I always knew what I wanted to do, but I was not sure how to become an astronaut."

Thomas knew there was a lot of competition to be an astronaut. Every year thousands applied for the chance, but few were selected.
"So, I knew that as a young boy, my only chance of becoming an astronaut was by working very hard in school every day," he stated. "Whatever I worked on, whatever I studied I always gave it my best effort. In high school, I got my bachelor's degree

in physics. The minimum degree one needed to be an astronaut then was a four-year college degree in math, science, engineering or a medical field."

Thomas graduated from Cleveland Heights High School in 1973. He went on to receive a Bachelor of Science degree in physics from Case Western Reserve University. Keeping in mind that competition for NASA was tight, Thomas stayed in school. He went to Cornell University and received a master's degree and Ph.D. in engineering. He then started work at AT&T doing research. With the education and practical experience, Thomas thought it was a good time to start applying to NASA for the astronaut program.

The first time he applied he was turned down. He was surprised but did not give up on his dream. The second time he was turned down, however, he became disheartened.

"At that point, I literally thought my grandmother and I had the same chance of becoming an astronaut, which was zero," he stated.

He decided to look closer at those who had been selected — looking at their education, background, and experience. Flight experience, though not required, was something most had. Others had skydiving and parachuting experience. He learned to do all three and even taught a university course.

The next time he sent in his application, he received an invitation from NASA to come to the Johnson Space Center for an interview. NASA even did a background check on him. However, again he was not selected.

"I was devastated," he sighed. "I thought I had made it in, but for the third time, NASA rejected me."

He decided it was time to give up. He told himself he would go to bed and the next day make a new plan for himself that didn't involve being an astronaut. There was just one problem.

"The next morning, the first thought that popped into my head was that I still wanted to be an astronaut," he realized. Thomas went back to looking at those who NASA selected and found that many already were working at Johnson Space Center. Wanting any edge he could get, Thomas quit his job and drove to Houston. He went to work for Lockheed Engineering and Science Company, where he reviewed materials for space shuttle payloads. A year later, he ended up being hired as a materials engineer at Johnson Space Center.

Thomas' focus was on the lifetime projections of advanced composite materials for use on Space Station Freedom. He also was a primary investigator for a crystal growth experiment that flew in space. He was working there when he decided to apply again to the astronaut program. This time he was accepted. Thomas vividly remembers the call from NASA telling him he was selected.

"I was jumping up and down, yelling," he recalled. "I was 35 years old when I got that call, and I started a four-year training program."

While Thomas was training to be an astronaut, he served NASA in other ways. He was involved in the safety, operations development, and payload branches of the astronaut office. Thomas also was the spacecraft shuttle communicator for three shuttle missions.

Thomas' first space flight was onboard the Space Shuttle Columbia on July 8, 1994. The shuttle was the second flight of the International Microgravity Laboratory. The fourteen-day mission had crew members conduct around-the clock research with more than 80 experiments.

Thomas was responsible for the orbital acceleration research experiment and several others involving the fundamentals of combustion ("in space, a flame is perfectly round," Thomas observed) and studied how the eggs of a salamander developed in zero gravity. He also worked on detailed test objectives, EVA, and took part in the amateur radio experiment. Thomas remarked that looking at the Earth from space really gives people a different perspective.

"How thin the atmosphere is; a thin blue line; how fragile our planet is and all would say that it changes your perspective on who you are," Thomas told the Lima News in 2023. "You gain a global perspective. We are all Earthlings."

The pace of the mission left for very little free time as the crew worked on the experiments.

"Each day, we performed 10-15 experiments," Thomas stated. "Some were fun to perform, others a bit tedious and boring. ... [The] mission was an extremely busy one, and each day we felt more and more fatigued."

The science operations were conducted around the clock with crew members designated into two teams, each working a 12-hour shift. By the time Columbia touched down on July 23, 1994, Thomas was ready to come home.

His next mission was as part of the all-Ohio crew of Discovery in July 1995. His experiences there led to a book he co-wrote with reporter Mike Bartell called Orbit of Discovery: The All-Ohio Space Shuttle Mission. The mission had the unusual distinction of being delayed because of a woodpecker. When the shuttle lifted off, there was a ruling that there would be no "woodpecker jokes' until the payload of the Tracking and Data Relay Satellite was deployed. The satellite was one of

Thomas' primary responsibilities on the flight. After it was deployed, the crew and Mission Control started in on the jokes.

"Just because you're 179 miles up doesn't mean you can get away from that little guy," laughed astronaut Story Musgrave sitting at Mission Control. "He's after you."

The jokes lasted throughout the mission, as anything that went wrong was blamed on the woodpecker. During the flight, Thomas got to speak to several students through the SAREX project as well as take part in experiments such as trying to produce a time-released antibiotic in weightlessness. He participated in Earth observations as well.

Thomas also brought a piece of home on the mission.

"When I went to space, I always tried to take a piece of Cleveland with me," he stated. "On my second flight, I took packs of Stadium Mustard. I had to take a little piece of Cleveland with me."

Discovery landed July 22, 1995. Less than six months later, Thomas was assigned another mission. Thomas would fly on the first flight of the microgravity science laboratory on board the Space Shuttle Columbia. Two months before the scheduled launch, Thomas broke his ankle during shuttle evacuation training. He didn't require surgery and continued training. NASA appointed a replacement just in case he wasn't better by liftoff.

Thomas did well in physical therapy and a few weeks before the launch, NASA decided to keep him on the mission. The day before the launch something unexpected that would be one of the highlights of Thomas' time at NASA occurred. He met his hero.

"Neil Armstrong was always my hero when I was growing up," he beamed. "We were both from the state of Ohio. So, I wrote to him and invited him to watch the launch of my third space shuttle, telling him I was an Ohio astronaut too. To my delight, he wrote back and said he would be there. I was so excited."

Armstrong came the day before the launch and met with Thomas and his wife for an hour, speaking to them and even taking pictures.

"I have been to space four times, but one of the most amazing things I have done in my life is spending that one-hour with Neil Armstrong," Thomas said.

Columbia launched on April 4, 1997, but the mission was cut short three days later after there were concerns about one of the fuel cells onboard. Thomas was prepared for a longer mission. The flight was to last sixteen days. He had packed a can of Tony Packo's Hot Dog Sauce from Toledo and even more Stadium Mustard in preparation.

Columbia returned to Earth on April 8, 1997, and NASA made the decision to fly the mission again less than three months later. It was the shortest turnaround in the shuttle program. Thomas' fourth mission would be onboard Columbia, which launched on July 1, 1997. It was to finish the Microgravity Science Laboratory Spacelab mission from his previous flight. During the nearly 16-day mission, Thomas again found himself on a team that would work 12 hours a day on experiments. He also again took part in the SAREX amateur radio experiment. Columbia landed July 17, 1997.

After his fourth flight, Thomas was named director of operations for NASA at the Gagarin Cosmonaut Training Center in Star City, Russia from 1999-2000. Thomas had been tapped for another mission that was to fly in late 2002. The mission was to go to ISS, however Thomas was pulled from the flight.

He had survived thyroid cancer 12 years earlier, but a doctor had concerns that the radiation he would experience onboard the space station could cause more cancer. Instead of returning to space, Thomas became a program scientist for ISS, where he oversaw experiments and science activities that would happen on the station.

Thomas retired from NASA in 2007. During his time at NASA, he earned several awards including the NASA Sustained Superior Performance Award, the NASA Distinguished Service Medal, two NASA Exceptional Service Medals, and four NASA Group Achievement Awards and NASA Space Flight Medals.

After his retirement, Thomas became the director of the Hackerman Academy of Mathematics and Science at Townson University. He continues to speak at various schools, organizations, and businesses. Thomas tells individuals he meets not to give up on their dreams — no matter how much hard work it takes.

"If you are willing to work hard, you can accomplish anything you want in your lifetime, just as I was able to," he stressed. "I went from this little boy dreaming to get into space to getting assigned on four missions."

Joy in the Journey: An aviation adventurer celebrating the exhilarating thirst of space exploration, all with a smile reflecting his spirit of discovery.

Gregory 'Box' Johnson

"Gregory 'Box' Johnson's story is a symphony of determination and inspiration, distinct from the musical legacy of his family, yet equally resonant. Born into a lineage of musicians, Johnson's childhood vision of moon landings and space exploration orchestrated a different path — one that led him to the stars. His journey from a young boy awestruck by the marvels of space travel to a pivotal role in the development and management of space research reflects a tenacity to pursue dreams, no matter how distant. Johnson's career, punctuated by significant contributions to space missions and a dedication to fostering scientific advancement, symbolizes the harmony between earthly beginnings and cosmic ambitions."

Gregory H. "Box" Johnson didn't march to the same beat as the rest of his family. Born into a family of musicians, a vision on a black-and-white television in his youth inspired him to play a different tune than the rest.

His father was an Air Force band leader, while his brother is a composer and church choir director. Johnson played trumpet and piano growing up. However, when he was young, he saw something that changed his life.

"I was 7 years old, watching a black-and-white television, when I watched Neil Armstrong step on the moon," Johnson said at the Summer Moon Festival in Wapakoneta in 2012. "I looked at my brother and sister and said, 'This is something I want to do when I grow up.'"

He added his parents had woken him and his siblings to watch the event while they were at his grandparents' house.

"That one singular event planted the seed of inspiration to me for the career path I took," he said, speaking with the Sakhikamva Foundation.

Gregory Johnson was born May 12, 1962, in South Ruislip, Middlesex in the United Kingdom, but considers Fairborn, Ohio, his hometown. Johnson graduated from Park Hills High School in Fairborn in 1980. He went on to receive his Bachelor of Science degree in aeronautical engineering from the U.S. Air Force Academy in 1984, then his master's degree in flight structures engineering from Columbia University in 1985. He later received his Master of Business Administration from the University of Texas, Austin.

After graduating from the U.S. Air Force Academy, Johnson was designated as a pilot at Reese Air Force Base. He then became a T-38A instructor pilot and was a F-15E Eagle pilot with the 335th Fighter Squadron. In 1990, he was deployed as part of Operation Desert Storm. He flew 34 combat missions there then an additional twenty-seven combat missions as part of Operation Southern Watch in Saudi Arabia. Johnson said a meeting with Charlie Bolden when he returned to the United States really was a pivotal moment in his life.

"A career is a conglomeration of all the different touchpoints in our lives," he stated. "Charlie Bolden was probably the single most important touchpoint that led me to the astronaut corps. While I had the dream of being an astronaut since I was 7, I really didn't think it was possible until I talked to this gentleman after he came back from the Hubble Telescope in 1993."

Johnson had asked Bolden if he really could become an astronaut. Bolden said it was possible; Johnson just needed to go to test pilot school and do well. The next week, he applied for test pilot school. In 1993, he completed Air Force Test Pilot School and was assigned to the 445th Flight Test Squadron. He test flew F-15C/E, NF-15B and T-13A/B aircraft. He then applied to NASA and in 1998 was selected to be an astronaut.

Prior to going into space, Johnson was assigned to the Shuttle Cockpit Avionics Upgrade Council, where he helped redesign cockpit displays for shuttle missions. With his expertise in flight structures, Johnson also served as the chief of shuttle abort planning and ascent procedure development. He also served as a technical assistant to the director of Flight Crew Operations Directorate.

His skills also placed him on several specialized technical teams tasked with solving and identifying issues. One of those teams dealt with the tragic Columbia disaster of 2003. Johnson's team proved that foam debris hitting the shuttle on ascent could "critically damage" the shuttle's thermal protection system.

Johnson was made the deputy chief of the Astronaut Safety Branch in 2004. In that capacity, he was charged with improving operational procedures and techniques to make astronauts feel safer in the space shuttle, ISS, and the T-38 jet. A year later, he was appointed as a crew representative to design and test NASA's Crew Exploration

Vehicle. A decade after being accepted into the astronaut program, Johnson went on his first mission. He was the pilot of the Endeavour Space Shuttle on its flight to the ISS.

"I won the lottery on this flight," Johnson told the Associated Press. "It's got the mission. It's got the crew. It's got everything. I wish my first mission came a little sooner. It's been an exercise of patience, but I'm really lucky, just amazingly lucky, to be on this flight."

To celebrate his first flight, Fairborn Primary Elementary School students sang a song about him on the day of the launch called "Fairborn's Hometown Hero." The song was written by teacher Stacey Frey and included the lyrics "If we all work hard in school, which all of us should do, when we grow up, we can be like Greg and fly the shuttle too."

Endeavour launched on March 11, 2008. Its mission was to deliver the Japanese Kibo Logistic Module and the Canadian Dextre robotics systems to the space station. The crew also took astronaut Garrett Reisman to the ISS and returned with Léopold Eyharts of the European Space Agency. During the fifteen-day mission, Johnson used the Canadarm2 to help spacewalkers, move the payload, and more. Johnson also used the robotic arm on the ISS to support the mission. He was responsible for the orbiter systems operations and helped dock and undock the shuttle from the ISS as well.

As part of the Endeavour crew, Johnson got a special surprise, as an original song written and sung by his brother, Gary, was played as a wake-up song for the crew. Johnson got another taste of home when students from Fairborn sent him questions to answer while he was in orbit. One question asked if he was excited or nervous.

"I was very excited and a little nervous before launch," he admitted. "The excitement came because it has been a dream of mine to fly in space since I was very young. I have been training for this specific mission for over a year and have been 'in training' at NASA for almost ten years. This is my first flight into space! I think being a little nervous is a natural reaction when one considers the incredible forces required to propel us into orbit."

Johnson later told students that "words can't describe" the experience of space.

The shuttle was attached to the ISS for twelve days before it undocked. Johnson then flew the shuttle around the station and fired the shuttle's jets to leave the area of the ISS.

"It's a very exciting time for a pilot," Johnson said, speaking at the post-flight presentation.

Endeavour returned to Earth on March 26, 2008. After returning, Johnson served as a capsule communicator for four flights. In 2009, Johnson retired from the U.S. Air Force as a colonel. During his time in the military, he was honored with a Legion of Merit, Distinguished Flying Cross, two Meritorious Service Medals, and four Air Medals.

Johnson was next scheduled to fly in 2011 as part of the Space Shuttle Endeavour crew. Crew members began training more than a year and a half before the mission. Tragedy struck the astronaut family the January prior to the mission, when fellow astronaut Mark Kelly's wife, U.S. Rep. Gabrielle Giffords, was shot in the head outside a supermarket in an assassination attempt. Johnson opened up his Houston home to the shuttle crew and their family.

"We wanted to deal with the emotions of all the kids," Johnson told the Associated Press. "My daughter was completely beside herself."

The six-member crew had fifteen children among them. The crew and their families had gotten close in the months leading up to the mission. The crew banded together as Giffords went through rehab with Kelly by her side. When Endeavour launched in May 2011, Giffords was able to attend. The mission would be Endeavour's last flight.

"We took some interesting payloads up into space. ... The Alpha Magnetic Spectrometer (AMS), probably one of the most significant experiments that have been on the space station. It's a particle detector to help us understand our universe," Johnson said of his last flight.

The mission also delivered critical supplies including communications antennas, a gas tank, and parts for the Dextre robot. The sixteen-day mission also dealt with station assembly and maintenance. Johnson was the lead robotic operator for both the space shuttle and station, helping install the AMS and Orbiter Boom Sensor System on the station. On the ISS, the crew was able to speak with the Pope — it was the first time the Vatican had called the space station.

"Space exploration is a fascinating scientific adventure," said Pope Benedict XVI. "I know you have been studying your equipment to further scientific research and to study radiation coming from outer space. But I think it is also an adventure of the human spirit. A powerful stimulus to reflect on the origins and the destiny of the universe and humanity."

The crew also had fun as well. They brought 13 Lego kits to the ISS. There, astronauts built Legos to see how they reacted in microgravity and shared results with schools as part of an educational program. Endeavour's crew also took along nutrition "STEM Bars" that were created by high school students Mikayla and

Shannon Diesch to raise awareness of STEM education. Johnson also took part in several interviews while on ISS. He was asked what he thought about the future of human spaceflight.

"I would love to be part of one of the future vehicles," he stated. "I would love to step on a planet." Johnson stated that commercial companies were working on new vehicles with "many interesting designs."

"That would interest me in flying one of those vehicles or being involved in the design of one of those future vehicles," he remarked. "I think in the next 50 years, we'll find space flight is quite commonplace. ...I'm hoping that space transportation will grow over the next five decades to a century and we will all be flying in space."

He also was asked if he looked at Earth any differently since he has been in space.

"When you look at the Earth from space you recognize how vast it is and how many different cultures and ecosystems there are," he observed. "You have to understand and appreciate how fragile the planet is."

Endeavour ended its more than fifteen-day mission and its last flight on June 1, 2011.

"Endeavour is near and dear to my heart," Johnson stated. "Flying my first flight with Endeavor and now flying the final flight of Endeavour, I feel very honored."

In late 2012, Johnson was selected as head of a visiting vehicles working group to help "plan, train and execute missions of Space X Dragon, Orbital Cygnus and JAXA HTV cargo vehicles to and from" the ISS. In 2013, Johnson retired from NASA. During his time there, he was honored with the NASA Exceptional Service Medal, two NASA Space Flight Medals, and NASA Superior Performance Awards.

"Greg contributed greatly to the constitution of the International Space Station, and I very much enjoyed my time in orbit with him," said Bob Behnken, chief of the Astronaut Office at NASA's Johnson Space Center about Johnson's retirement.

Johnson left NASA to become the president and executive director of the Center for the Advancement of Science in Space, a nonprofit organization whose mission is to improve life on Earth through the development and management of research and development and communicating the value of the ISS, which includes STEM education.

"The space station is a bright shiny object that we can use to accelerate learning and inspire the next generation of science, astronauts, and engineers," Johnson stated during a presentation at the International Symposium for Personal and Commercial Spaceflight in 2015.

A Giant Leap: A historical moment of space exploration, reminding us of the monumental steps taken by astronauts on behalf of humanity.

Michael 'Bueno' Good

"Michael 'Bueno' Good's journey as an astronaut is a tale of relentless ambition and joyful exploration. Good's childhood fascination with aerospace, nurtured through visits to air museums, propelled him towards a career that transcended the Earth's bounds. His journey from Ohio to orbit symbolizes the power of dreams and the fun that accompanies their pursuit.
Good's missions with NASA — filled with both challenging spacewalks and light-hearted moments like pitching at a baseball game and floating with a Cavaliers jersey in space — highlight the blend of professionalism and playfulness in his spacefaring adventures.
His story is a testament to the belief that reaching for the stars can be as exhilarating as it is inspiring, proving that the universe is not just a place for rigorous scientific endeavor, but also a playground for the human spirit."

Being an astronaut is a lot of hard work, but it's also a lot of fun. Michael "Bueno" Good has a lot of stories to tell about his time as an astronaut and the fun he had.

Good was born Oct. 13, 1962, in Parma, Ohio, though he considers Broadview Heights his home. Growing up, Good and his family would visit air museums, which helped him develop a love of aerospace.

"I really love air museums and I remember coming here [to the National Museum of the Air Force] as a kid, and it is one of the things that inspired me to study aerospace engineering and get into the business," Good told the crowd during an event to open the Crew Compartment Training exhibit in 2012.

In 1980, Good graduated from Brecksville-Broadview Heights High School. He went on to receive a Bachelor of Science in aerospace engineering in 1984 and a Master of Science in aerospace engineering in 1986, both from University of Notre

Dame. Good was a member of Notre Dame's ROTC. Before completing his master's degree, Good earned a commission as a second lieutenant in the U.S. Air Force.

"I was in engineering but made the decision to go into aerospace engineering in 1981, which was the first year that the space shuttle flew so that definitely had an influence on me too. I watched that and said 'you know this is something I'd like to be a part of,'" Good recalled during an interview for the University of Notre Dame.

After receiving his degrees, Good became a flight test engineer at Elgin Air Force Base and then was assigned to the Tactical Air Warfare Center. Good served as a flight test engineer for the Ground Launched Cruise Missile program. In 1989, he received his wings.

He participated in lead-in flight and F-111 transition training. Good was then assigned to the 20th Fighter Wing, where he served as an F-111 instructor weapon system officer. In 1993, he was selected for test pilot school, graduating in 1994. He then was assigned to the 420 Flight Test Squadron. With the squadron, Good test flew the B-2 Stealth Bomber. Later, Good attended the Air Command and Staff College. He was assigned to the 46th Operation Support Squadron, where he served as operations officer and F-15 test weapons system officer. Good then decided to apply to be an astronaut.

"I just remember the interview," he told the 2 Funny Astronauts podcast. "We went down to Johnson Space Center for a whole week. It was mostly medical and physiological testing too."
The 45-minute interview astronauts went through was headed by John Young, an astronaut veteran who had flown with the Gemini, Apollo, and space shuttle programs.

"That 45-minute interview with John Young at the head of the table and the icon he was. ... I don't know what my heart rate was. I just remember looking at him. He didn't even say, 'Hi Mike how are you doing?' He just got right into it. He says, 'Alright Mike, tell us everything about yourself starting after high school.' Boom. Go. One question, 45 minutes."

Good must have done well, as NASA selected him to be part of the astronaut program in 2000. Before his first mission to space, Good had technical duties in the Advanced Vehicles and Space Shuttle branches. Good joked that one of the reasons he wanted to be an astronaut was just so he could throw out the first pitch of a baseball game.

"I'm a big Cleveland Indians fan and wanted to throw out a first pitch at an Indians game," he recalled. "Actually, my family knows the Dolans, who own the Cleveland Indians. After I got selected to be an astronaut I told [Mr. Dolan], 'Hey, my dream is to throw out a pitch at a Cleveland Indians game' and he says, 'Have you ever flown in space?' I said no. He said, 'Call me when you fly in space.'"

It was nine years before that happened. Good kept that in mind as he continued his astronaut training. Good's first mission was on Atlantis on the final space shuttle mission to repair and upgrade the Hubble Space Telescope.

"I think the Hubble mission was my most challenging mission," Good admitted during an interview for the Smithsonian National Air and Space Museum. "There was just so much to it. It was my first spaceflight mission and it was my first spacewalk. So there was a lot to learn. We were really well prepared though and really well trained. It was probably the most fun I've ever had — just training to go on the mission. To actually fly it was icing on the cake."

Good was able to throw out the first pitch at an Orioles game prior to flying. The entire crew of Atlantis was invited to throw out a pitch and Good, who pitched in high school, was selected to pitch for the crew. Before the game, crew members were driving from the hotel to Goddard Space Flight Center and went to a high school, as Good wanted to practice pitching from the mound. The baseball team was practicing though, so Good approached the coach.

"I said, 'Hey I'm throwing the first pitch at the Orioles game, can I throw a couple to your guys at batting practice?' He said, 'Sure, that's great,'" Good recalled. "I'm throwing batting practice to a high school team. It all paid off that night at the game; I did well. I didn't bounce it in. I think it was a strike."

He had thrown out a first pitch, but his astronaut work was just beginning. Atlantis launched on May 11, 2009, for its nearly thirteen-day mission. During the mission Good and fellow astronaut Michael Massimino replaced Hubble's gyroscopes, which help the telescope point and hold on a target. The duo also would repair the Space Telescope Imaging Spectrograph, also known as the power supply system.

"It's just nice to be part of this," Good stated to Cleveland.com. "It's just a really special mission."

Good took a piece of home with him on the flight — a Notre Dame banner — which he presented to the college later that year. Atlantis landed on May 24, 2009. Good, however, had lost something on the shuttle.

"I flew on Atlantis twice, but my glasses flew on Atlantis three times. I lost my glasses on the Hubble mission. They floated off because up in space you don't have to put things down on the table, you just let go of them," he explained. "I let go of them, come back and they were gone. I searched everywhere. I couldn't find them."

Once they landed, he informed the ground crew that he lost his glasses somewhere on the shuttle. The ground crew couldn't find them either.

"The shuttle flies again on the next mission ... and then that one comes down," he said. "They [the ground crew] find a bunch of stuff behind the dashboard in one of the fans for the displays. They show me this picture and there's glasses. There's pens, ear plugs. ... I get an email of a picture of all this stuff and they go, 'Are those your glasses?'"

Good was able to get his glasses back in time for his next mission. Upon returning to Earth, Good also remembered to ask Dolan to let him throw out a first pitch.

"He said yes and was very gracious," Good exclaimed. "It was pretty cool when I got to do it. My mom and dad were there, all my high school buddies."

Good had a very busy year in 2009 as he also retired from the U.S. Air Force as a colonel. During his time in the military, he was honored with the Legion of Merit, Air Force Commendation Medal, Air Force Achievement Medal, Combat Readiness Medal, four Meritorious Service Medals, and two Aerial Achievement Medals.

Good's second flight was onboard the Space Shuttle Atlantis, which launched May 14, 2010. Originally, Good was not assigned to the mission. He replaced Karen Nyberg, who suffered a temporary medical condition and could not take part. The primary payloads on the flight were the Russian mini-research module and Integrated Cargo Carrier Vertical Light Deployable for the ISS. Atlantis docked with the ISS on May 16, 2000.

During the mission, Good took part in two spacewalks. The first was to replace four of the six batteries attached to the ISS truss and to fix a snagged cable on the ISS Orbiter Boom Sensor System. The second spacewalk was to connect a liquid ammonia jumper hose, replace the other two batteries on the ISS truss, transfer a grapple fixture, and prepare for future spacewalks. Good remembered being at the end of one of his spacewalks with Garrett Reisman and being asked to go get something out of the shuttle's payload bay. Good then got an idea.

"I said, 'Ah ha. This is going to be an opportunity. This is going to be fun,'" Good said, adding that on his previous mission he could scramble to the back windows of the aft of the flight deck to get pictures taken. He told Reisman to be quiet when they got into the payload bay.

"We don't want ground to hear us and yell at us for not doing what we're supposed to be doing," he joked. "So I said, 'We're going to go up to those windows and get our picture taken.' So it was just awesome. We climbed down off the station across the nose of the shuttle and we go down into the payload bay and we popped up at those two back windows."

The picture ended up on the front page of the New York Times, which Good enjoyed.

"It was pretty cool," he said, adding that while fellow astronauts were taking their picture, they took pictures of those inside the shuttle as well.

The crew of Atlantis had fun in other ways too. They spoke to comedian Stephen Colbert during the flight. Colbert had made a joke about the crew replacing the batteries on the space station:
"What does it run on, like AAs?" he quipped. Good had to inform him the batteries were about 400 pounds apiece — not quite double A's.

"We had to do quite a lot of working out at the gym before those spacewalks," Good joked.

Good said his two missions were very different.

"[It was] a totally different experience going out of the airlock at the international space station," he stated. "There was a lot of room to float around. There's so much room there to go through the labs and different modules."

While he enjoyed his time on ISS, Good also remembered everyone back home. On his cuff checklist for the mission, Good kept a reminder.

"I put a big ND for Notre Dame on my cuff checklist," he said. "Part of flying into space is being able to take people with you. That's a little way to take people with you. All my friends from Notre Dame, I know they were following me. I actually had an email log going with them so I would send emails from space to my classmates."

He said some pictures were taken from space that showed the ND on there. Good even took a Cleveland Cavs jersey up to space on the mission and brought it back. The jersey had the mission number (132) on it. He presented it to the Cavs organization on Nov. 13, 2010.

The ISS mission was to be the last for the Space Shuttle Atlantis. It touched down on May 26, 2010.

"She's a great ship. It was a real honor to be on the last flight," Good said during a post-flight interview. "Atlantis treated us pretty well. She's just an incredible ship. She just worked perfectly."

Atlantis ended up making one final flight in 2011. The shuttle was then retired to the Kennedy Space Center Visitor Complex in Florida.

"I like to visit Atlantis at the Kennedy Space Center," Good said.

After his two missions, Good served as NASA's liaison to the Air Force Space Command and on the Commercial Crew Program as assistant to the program manager for crew operations and testing. In his role with the Commercial Crew Program, he helped SpaceX and Boeing to prepare to launch astronauts to the ISS. Good admitted it was tough to say goodbye to the space shuttles.

"The shuttle's been such an incredible vehicle," he stated. "It has the capacity like no other."

He touched on the need to continue to explore space.

"We need to go to the moon, Mars, asteroids," Good told the science blog Lofty Ambitions. "Search out other destinations. ... I think we as a county and as an international partnership it may turn out to be we can get there. We will develop the technology to do it safely and bring them back."

In 2019, Good retired from NASA.

"Mike's vision and execution for the Commercial Crew Program's Joint Test Team has been critical to the maturing of each of the provider's crew cabins," said Kathy Lueders, Commercial Crew Program manager, of Good's retirement. "Mike had the dream of bringing the best of NASA to work side by side with the best of Boeing and SpaceX to find the safest and most practical solutions to the inevitable trades that need to be made. His leadership will be sorely missed but he set the right trajectory for us and now it will be our job to make him proud."

Good currently is the director of crew integration for Blue Origin. NASA has selected Blue Origin as a contractor "to develop a human landing system for the agency's Artemis V mission to the Moon."

Generations of Dreams: One man's legacy as an inspiring place explorer nurturing the dreams of future generations.

Michael Foreman

"Michael Foreman's story, from the small town of Wadsworth, to the vast expanse of space, is a journey of unwavering determination and inspiring achievement. Igniting his dream to become an astronaut at the tender age of 8, Foreman charted a course that defied the conventional expectations of his family. His path, marked by repeated applications to NASA and an unrelenting commitment to his goal, culminated in a remarkable career that saw him leave his footprints in the cosmos. Foreman's tale is a vivid reminder of the power of perseverance and the importance of pursuing one's passions, no matter the odds. Through his spacewalks and work on the International Space Station, he not only contributed significantly to our understanding of space but also brought a touch of his Ohio roots to the stars. His story is a beacon of hope and inspiration, encouraging all to dream big and to tirelessly chase those dreams."

Michael Foreman's mother wanted him to be a doctor, but he had more stellar ambitions.

"My mother was a nurse. I remember my mother sitting me down one day and saying 'Mike you know what you ought to do one day. You ought to go to MIT and become a doctor.' ... A lot of mothers at that time wanted their kids to be doctors. I don't know where she got the MIT part. I didn't like the sight of blood. I wanted to go to the Naval Academy and be an astronaut," he told the Associated Press in an interview.

Foreman was born March 2, 1957, in Columbus, but considers Wadsworth, Ohio, where he graduated high school in 1975, his hometown. Foreman knew he wanted to be an astronaut when he was 8. Interesting enough, the number eight would mean a lot throughout his life.

"I started to follow the space program and read some books about the early astronauts and just decided that's what I wanted to do," he recalled. Foreman also jokes about Ohio having so many astronauts.

"People ask me all the time why there are so many astronauts from Ohio," he remarked, speaking at the Champaign Library. "Of course, I tell them, 'It's just a lot of people looking for work outside of the state.' The truth is, coincidentally, [that] John Glenn, Neil Armstrong, Jim Lovell from Apollo 13 were all in the first three classes of astronauts so when Ohioans started doing astronaut things, the news media in Ohio picked up on it so I heard a lot about it — the space program. A lot of us said, 'That looks like a cool job.'"

Foreman remembers reading the book We Seven, which detailed how the original seven astronauts got into the program.

"I found out four out of the original seven were naval aviators," he remembered. At 8, Foreman thought all he had to do was be a navy aviator to be an astronaut. He told his parents about his plans and his dad suggested he think about the Naval Academy. Foreman wrote to the academy, which sent him a catalog with some information.

"It had pictures of guys playing every sport imaginable," Foreman stated. "I said, 'Yeah Dad, this looks like summer camp. I want to go there. It looks great.' ... I dedicated myself to getting good grades and got into the Naval Academy."

Foreman attended the U.S. Naval Academy, graduating with a Bachelor of Science degree in aerospace engineering in 1979 and then a Master of Science degree in aeronautical engineering in 1986. Foreman sent in his first application to NASA as a grad student but was rejected.

"I thought, 'I haven't been to test pilot school,'" he said. "I was not deterred at that point."

Foreman applied eight times for test pilot school before he was accepted in 1989. He had a lot to do while he applied. He became a naval aviator in 1981. He went on to become the assistant air operations officer on the USS Coral Sea. He then was assigned to the Force Warfare Aircraft Test Directorate. Later, he was reassigned as a flight instructor and operations officer at the U.S. Naval Test Pilot School. In 1993, he became a deputy then chief engineer for the T-45 Goshawk aircraft program at Naval Air Systems Command in Virginia. All the while, Foreman kept applying for the astronaut program.

He continued working and became the military director for the Naval Air Warfare Center Aircraft Division's research and engineering group. He also was assigned as the Navy's liaison to NASA's Johnson Space Center. He was working as a technical lead for an advanced orbiter cockpit project team, when he heard he had been accepted into the astronaut program. Foreman had applied to NASA to be part of the astronaut program eight times.

"Perseverance means everything," he said. "You have to find something that you love and if you continue to try, you will become successful."

Foreman has spoken to students at various schools about this drive to become an astronaut.

"I never gave up on my dream of going to space, even when I was rejected, and I kept trying over and over," he said in a meeting with students at Space Camp Turkiye. "Dream big and set goals in life, but remember that if you reach your goals in your first try, your goals may not be high enough. Do something every day to achieve your goal. Don't give up any of your dreams."

Before his first flight, Foreman was assigned technical duties that included representing the astronaut office on training issues, being a liaison between the Space Shuttle Branch and both Johnson Space Center and Kennedy Space Center. He also served as deputy of the Space Shuttle Branch. Foreman's first space mission was on board the Endeavour. He was a mission specialist during the flight, which lifted off on March 11, 2008.

"It's a pretty wild ride," Foreman later recalled of his first launch. "It's a four and half million-pound vehicle with seven and half million pounds of thrust, so when those solid rocket boosters light off, you know you're going somewhere."

The crew delivered the Japanese Experimental Logistics Module as well as the Dextre Robotic System to the International Space Station. The mission also left astronaut Garrett Reisman at the station, while bringing European astronaut Léopold Eyharts back to Earth. Foreman said ironically, he had always wanted to go into space, but the first thing he did up in space was look back toward Earth.

"It's beautiful," he said. "You can't stop looking at the Earth. The views are amazing."

Foreman performed three space walks during the mission. He also acted as the intravehicular officer. He helped assemble and outfit the Dextre, and replace a failed remote power control module on the station.

There was a little bit of trouble with the Dextre, as two of the latches for one of the robotic arms wouldn't release until Foreman and fellow astronaut Richard Linnehan used pry bars. Foreman also took time out to inspect a jammed rotating joint that had restricted some solar wings.

He also took part in a heat shield repair demonstration. Foreman and fellow astronaut Robert Behnken used a caulking gun and patching material to work on damaged space shuttle thermal tiles that had been brought onboard the shuttle. The tools for the repair demonstration were made following the 2003 Columbia disaster that occurred because of damage to the tiles from foam insulation striking a wing.

In addition to the spacewalks, Foreman provided intravehicular support for two other spacewalks.

Endeavour landed after its more than fifteen-day mission on March 26, 2008. Returning home, Foreman served as the chief of external programs at the Glenn Research Center. He then was assigned to the exploration branch, where he worked on the Commercial Crew Development Program.

Before his next flight, Foreman retired from the U.S. Navy. During his time in the military, he earned a Legion of Merit, Defense Meritorious Service Medal, Meritorious Service Medal, Navy Commendation Medal, and the Navy Achievement Medal.

His next mission took him to the International Space Station. The shuttle Atlantis lifted off on Nov. 16, 2009. The crew delivered two Express Logistics Carriers as well as replacement parts for the station's power system. They also took astronaut Nicole Stott back to Earth from the ISS. Foreman acted as lead spacewalker on the mission. He completed two spacewalks during the mission and kept a piece of home with him each time he went out.

"My cuff checklist said go Navy beat Army," he said of his EVA suit.

During the mission, Foreman helped transfer a spare antenna from Atlantis to the station's thrust, maintain the Kibo laboratory's robotic arm, install a grappling adaptor to an assembly, secure the Orbiter Boom Sensor System, install cables (and troubleshoot any connector issues), and work on the protective shield outside the module. He also helped install a wireless video system external transceiver assembly.

The mission was a success despite the fact that there were false fire and decompression alarms that went off during the mission that woke up Foreman and fellow astronaut Randolph Bresnik the night before one of their spacewalks.

Foreman had a lot of fun on his second mission. He even joked "I can see my house from here," as the shuttle was over Houston, which was cloud-covered at the time. During one of his spacewalks, Foreman had to be thinking about the crowbar from his first mission after he and fellow astronaut Robert Satcher ran into a problem deploying a payload mounting mechanism on the station's solar power truss. They could not get a tight bolt free. Eventually, the duo used a rubber-tipped hammer to strike the bolt while jiggling the mechanism to set it free. Later, the two were in charge of taking care of some latching end effectors for robot arms. The latching systems used snares to lock onto a payload's grappling fixture, and there had been issues with them in the past.

"He'll [Satcher] go and apply some grease to the snares inside those latching end effectors to make sure that they don't have a problem later in life," Foreman said. "So he's doing some preventive maintenance basically on those while I do that spare cable task."

Foreman also removed a safety slide wire that was no longer being used. The crew did a lot of work before departing.

"Hopefully, we came and left the station in a better place than what it was before we got here," Foreman said as he radioed after the last EVA from inside the station complex on Nov. 23, 2009.

After his second flight, Foreman became chief of external programs at the Glenn Research Center in Cleveland from 2010-11. He then served as the safety branch chief in NASA's astronaut office, supporting the exploration branch and working with the Commercial Crew Development Program. Foreman retired from NASA in 2015.

"Mike is a great American who has served our nation for 35 years," said Chris Cassidy, chief of the Astronaut Office at NASA's Johnson Space Center in Houston. "We have been lucky to have him as part of our NASA team, and wish him and his family the best."

After retiring from NASA, Foreman joined a construction project and consulting firm called Venturi Outcomes LLC. In 2016, he was elected to the city council in Friendswood, Texas, where he would later become mayor. He still holds that post in the city. On Friendswood's website, Foreman urges everyone to dream big.

"Strive to make each ordinary day become extraordinary," he said. "Take a moment to not only count your blessings ... but think about the opportunities ahead, and dream big!"

Foreman still speaks to students about his time in the space program, hoping to inspire them like Armstrong and Glenn inspired him.

"I hope we can inspire them to pursue a degree in science and engineering, maybe even decide to be an astronaut one day," Foreman urged.

Voyage Beyond: A tribute to the brave explorer who has ventured into the great unknown, marked by his unique blend of human determination and the mechanics of exploration.

Thomas Hennen

"Thomas Hennen's remarkable journey from Groveport to the stars is a testament to the synergy of military precision and space exploration. As the first military imagery specialist and the only warrant officer from the Department of Defense to venture into space, Hennen's unique career path is a blend of intense dedication, specialized intelligence expertise, and the pioneering spirit of space travel. His pivotal role in the Military Man in Space program aboard the Space Shuttle Atlantis in 1991 highlights the crucial intersection of military strategy and space technology. Hennen's narrative is not just a story of technical achievements; it's a thrilling adventure that showcases the uncharted territories that await at the confluence of military intelligence and astronautics."

Thomas Hennen can't tell you everything he did while at NASA; some of it's still classified. Hennen remains the first military imagery specialist to fly on a space shuttle and the only warrant officer in the Department of Defense to go into space.

Hennen was born Aug. 17, 1952, in Albany, Ga., but considers Columbus, Ohio, his hometown. He graduated from Groveport-Madison High School in Groveport, Ohio, in 1970, and went on to attend Urbana College for two years. In 1972, he joined the U.S. Army as an imagery intelligence analyst (IMINT). In 1973, he completed his U.S. Army Imagery Interpretation course and U.S. Army Administrative Specialist course. He took several more classes, including ones for intelligence officers, through the U.S. Army, Marines and Air Force.

From 1973-75, Hennen was assigned to the 163rd Military Intelligence Battalion out of Fort Hood. There he helped plan, develop, and conduct several tests and evaluations for combat such as new camouflage, remote piloted vehicles, effectiveness of firing methods for the AH-1 Cobra helicopter, and more. Later, he was assigned to the 203rd Military Intelligence Detachment, serving as the operations non-commissioned officer and chief of the tactical and strategic exploitation divisions. From 1978-81, Hennen was assigned to the 497th

Reconnaissance Technical Group in Germany. In that assignment, he was to support the office of the Deputy Chief of Staff for Intelligence.

In 1981, Hennen was appointed a warrant officer. He moved to the U.S. Army Intelligence Center and School in Arizona, where he spent the next four years. According to the U.S. Army, Hennen "quickly became the Army's definitive authority on advanced technical IMINT collection capabilities, authoring the Army's Radar Imagery Training Plan, helping develop the TENCAP [Tactical Exploitation of National Capabilities Program] Systems Management Model, and completing the entire Instructional Systems Development process for five critical intelligence programs."

In addition, he helped develop imagery space intelligence training and managed a classified IMINT project for the office of the Secretary of Defense. In 1986, Hennen was tapped to be Maj. Gen. Julius Parker Jr.'s representative to the U.S. Army Space Program Office in Washington, D.C. In that capacity, Hennen managed more than $2 billion in classified intelligence collection programs and served on multiple groups and subcommittees for developing policies on space-based intelligence collection.

Hennen was then named to be an astronaut payload specialist for the Pentagon's Military Man in Space program in 1988. NASA confirmed that as it selected Hennen to be a payload specialist in 1989. His first and only flight was onboard the Space Shuttle Atlantis in 1991.

Atlantis launched on Nov. 24, 1991, after being delayed for five days due to a malfunctioning unit on a booster. On launch day, it was delayed for thirteen minutes to allow an orbiting spacecraft to pass the area.

According to the U.S. Army, Hennen performed experiments "to advance military strategy for operations in space." The experiments included testing the effects on the human body of living and working in space for long periods of time. He also used his IMINT experience to conduct the Terra Scout experiment using cameras, sensors, and a specialized folded optical telescope known as the Spaceborne Direct View Optical System. Hennen took photos and video of various ground and sea targets and analyzed them in space before relaying information to ground commanders.

"His determination of what could actually be seen from space was critical to informing the DD space-based geospatial intelligence collection and analysis strategy for the next several decades," according to information from the U.S. Army.

Hennen previously had studied the sites he was to observe. Each of the selected sites had a package with maps, photographs, and large resolution panels that were to help assess resolution limits from space. According to information from the U.S. Army, on the third day of the mission Hennen focused on sites in Learmouth, Australia, and Ford Island, Hawaii. An error with the Spaceborne Direct-View Optical System and weather caused observations to be postponed to four other sites.

With the optical system problem somewhat fixed, Hennen was later able to observe sites in South Africa, the Indian Ocean, and Malaysia. Hennen was supposed to observe several other sites including Brisbane, Australia; Cape Canaveral, Fla.; Pearl Harbor, Hawaii; the U.S. Embassy in Manila, the Philippines; Midway Island; Christmas Island; Chase Field, Texas; Honduras; the Strait of Malacca; and Yucatan, Mexico. Poor weather conditions, however, made it difficult to see some of the targets. At the time, the list of sites to be observed was not released to the public.

"The techniques we use in our data collection operations in the military, we certainly don't want to give that to other people," Hennen stated to the Associated Press in 1991.

Regardless of the issues, the Army deemed the mission a success because it gathered important information on not only the skillsets people need, but the equipment and how they can be best used for various intelligence aspects.

During the flight, the crew spoke to reporters. One asked Hennen what human observers in space could do that satellites could not do better.

"My portion of the Military Man in Space is more in the area of research and development, not trying to add on to the current tactical situation that I'm observing on the shuttle," he answered. "My particular experiment kind of characterizes how a human observes this particular environment and try to translate that later on to unmanned sensing devices so we won't have a specific man in the loop as you will in orbit. That particular work has a long way to go. This is the first step in this endeavor."

He then was asked if there were any observations that surprised him as he worked in space.

"I think quite a few. The work I did before has never been from this vantage point. I think [that is] one of the biggest things that helps the observation, even with the naked eye, and let me just say before going any further we're not trying to compete with any existing equipment that's out there with the equipment we've brought onboard Atlantis with this mission," he stated. "We're just going to characterize a variety of different observation techniques and skills and ways of doing business."

Hennen said that the color from the vantage point of space was wonderful.

"We just don't seem to get the tonal qualities that you get with return fill-based or electro-optical or digital type of products," he remarked. "They just don't seem to have the same color properties as you have here with your naked eye right outside the shuttle window. So probably color is the biggest factor that I really hadn't anticipated."

The mission wasn't all work. Hennen said he had "a great time" in space. With the mission happening over the Thanksgiving holiday, the crew had a holiday dinner in space. Video taken onboard shows all six men in the lower deck area enjoying what fellow astronaut Mario Runco described as "a scrumptious meal of turkey and gravy, some noodles. We had fresh cranberry sauce and some pumpkin delight, all the fixings of a traditional Thanksgiving."

The mission was to last longer than it did, but NASA ordered Atlantis to return home after one of three navigational units onboard failed. The flight was cut short by three days, and Atlantis touched back down on Earth on Dec. 1, 1991.

Hennen was assigned to NASA for five years before he retired from the U.S. Army on Nov. 30, 1995. During his time in the military, he was awarded the Defense Superior Service Medal, Legion of Merit, Army Commendation Medal, Military Intelligence Corps Association's Knowlton Award, Meritorious Service Medal with two Oak Leaf Clusters, Army Achievement Medal with one Oak Leaf Cluster, Armed Forces Space and Missile Badge Senior Level, and Army Aviation Badge with Astronaut Device. He also earned a NASA Space Flight Medal.

After leaving NASA, Hennen was the executive director of the Atlantis Foundation, a nonprofit that aids individuals with developmental disabilities. It was a position he kept until August 2008, when he left to become an independent consultant. In 2002, Hennen was inducted into the Military Intelligence Hall of Fame.

Honorary Buckeye Astronauts

These individuals may not have been born or grew up in Ohio, but have spent significant time in or have worked to promote and enhance opportunities in the Buckeye State, or have had proclamations declaring them state citizens for their efforts.

Space Sentinels: A salute to the guardian of the cosmos who walk among us. She intertwines the beauty of celestial discovery with the valor of one who's explored it.

Kathryn Sullivan

"Kathryn Sullivan is a trailblazer in both space and ocean exploration. As the first American woman to conduct a spacewalk and the first woman to dive to Challenger Deep, Sullivan's diverse career, spanning roles as a geologist, astronaut, and influential policy maker, showcase her significant impact on science and technology. Her tenure at NASA and recognition by Time magazine and John Glenn are testaments to her wide-reaching influence. Sullivan's adventurous and innovative spirit highlights the possibilities beyond traditional paths, inspiring future generations of explorers and scientists."

The first American woman to walk in space is also the first woman to dive to Challenger Deep, the deepest known part of Earth's seabed. She's gone from studying geology to becoming an astronaut to promoting policies on science and technology.

"I have no fear of veering from the straight path," Kathryn Sullivan explained when she received an honorary Doctorate of Public Affairs at Ohio State University.

Sullivan also has lived in a lot of places in her life. She was born in New Jersey, but has lived in California, Canada, and Ohio. NASA's own Ohio astronaut graphic even lists Sullivan among the state's space walkers.

Sullivan served as the first executive director of Ohio State's Battelle Center for Science, Engineering and Public Policy. She was the president and chief executive officer of COSI in Columbus from 1996-2006. She also was an adjunct professor of geology at The Ohio State University.

Her ties to Ohio are strong, but her connection to the whole Earth is what helps drive her. In 2014, Sullivan was named one of the top 100 most influential people in the world by Time magazine. John Glenn even contributed to the article about her, stating that Sullivan was "not just an ivory-tower scientist."

"She was part of NASA's first class of female astronauts ... and went on to fly three shuttle missions," Glenn wrote. "She is the first American woman to walk in space and served aboard the mission that deployed the Hubble Space Telescope. That role in helping humanity look outward has not prevented her from looking homeward. The planet is suffering increasingly severe upheavals, at least partly as a result of climate change .... I believe my good friend Kathy is the right person for the right job at the right time."

Sullivan was born Oct. 3, 1951, in New Jersey. Her father was an aerospace engineer and moved the family to California when she was young to be closer to aerospace activities in the 1960s. Sputnik launched when she was six. Airplanes were suddenly all around, with her father joining a flying club. Then NASA was founded, and National Geographic started running articles about space.

"I think that general sense of amazing adventure afoot in the world and getting glimpses of it was really what entranced me, and I think that at some deep level this set a strong sense of wanting to be part of such adventures," Sullivan told the Johnson Space Center's Oral History Project. "There are people who get to do these amazing adventures, and that clearly would be really cool. Just that feeling of what it must be like to be part of things like this was very compelling and very moving."

When she was in first grade, Sullivan had a classmate that was also a future astronaut: Sally Ride.

Sullivan graduated from William Howard Taft High School in Los Angeles in 1969. She then attended the University of California, Santa Cruz, earning a Bachelor of Science degree in earth sciences in 1973. Five years later she earned her Doctor of Philosophy in geology from Dalhousie University. During her time at Dalhousie, she also took part in several expeditions to study the sea floors of both the Atlantic and Pacific oceans. She had planned a career in oceanography.

In 1976, Sullivan went home for Christmas with her family. It was there her brother, Grant, told her NASA was looking for a new group of astronauts. He had applied and urged her to do it too. At the time, they teased each other about it. When she returned to school, however, she saw an ad from NASA about their recruitment.

"When I read that, a different gear clicked," she recalled. "I recognized a strong parallel between the mission specialist role, as they described it, and the oceanographic expeditions."

Sullivan decided to apply after weighing all her options. She continued putting her Ph.D. dissertation together, and even got a call about her postdoctoral work doing deep-sea marine geology. She told them she would take it as long as she didn't hear back from NASA. The call then came from NASA. They asked her to come in for an interview. Sullivan ended up being one of the six women selected as an astronaut in NASA's 1978 class.

Her research interests at NASA focused on remote sensing. In addition to her astronaut training, she also earned her pilot's license in 1979. Sullivan's first trip to space was onboard the Space Shuttle Challenger in October 1984. The nearly eight-day mission was the first flight with two women, as Ride also was onboard. Sullivan took her first spacewalk during the mission. She, along with astronaut David Leestma, installed a valve assembly into simulated satellite propulsion plumbing to see if it was possible to do satellite refueling during a spacewalk.

"Our commander Bob Crippen actually ordered us to stop for a minute and pivot away from the space shuttle and look around," she said. "And he said, 'Take in the fact that you're 190 miles above the Earth, you're doing 17,500 miles an hour. ... You're actually really here.' I was forever grateful he did that."

Sullivan's next mission was to deploy the Hubble Space Telescope in 1986. However, the Challenger disaster in January of that year canceled the mission. It wasn't until four years later that mission would resume. During those four years, Sullivan joined the U.S. Naval Reserve as an oceanography officer. In 1988, she was commissioned with the rank of lieutenant commander. She also worked as a capsule communicator for several missions.

The Hubble mission would happen in April 1990. During five days in space, the crew deployed the Hubble Space Telescope and conducted experiments including some on weightlessness and magnetic fields. They also conducted Earth observations. Sullivan wrote a book about her life and experiences with the Hubble telescope called Handprints on Hubble, which was published in 2019.

Sullivan's last space mission was on the Shuttle Atlantis in 1992. During the nine-day mission, the crew took the Atmospheric Laboratory for Applications and Science (ATLAS) on to Spacelab and conducted studies in atmospheric chemistry, solar radiation, space plasma physics, and ultraviolet astronomy. Atlantis crews were split into two teams, each working 12-hour shifts to conduct the experiments. Sullivan had the responsibility of a dose-response experiment to record the luminosity in the upper atmosphere when an electron pulse was fired at it from space. Sullivan also took part in the SAREX radio experiment.

In 1993, Sullivan left NASA when she accepted a presidential appointment of Chief Scientist at the National Oceanic and Atmospheric Administration (NOAA). In that capacity, she oversaw various research and technology programs that dealt with climate change, satellites, and marine biodiversity. A decade later she served as the acting NOAA administrator. In 1994, she was confirmed as the Under Secretary of Commerce for Oceans and Atmosphere as well as NOAA administrator. She then was appointed as a member of President Joe Biden's Council of Advisors on Science and Technology.

Sullivan also returned to her love of the ocean. In 2020, she went onboard an EYOS Expedition to reach Challenge Deep — a 35,810-foot descent into the ocean. When she got back to the surface, Sullivan made a special phone call to the ISS to talk about the experience.

"As a hybrid oceanographer and astronaut this was an extraordinary day, a once in a lifetime day, seeing the landscape of the Challenger Deep and then comparing notes with my colleagues on the ISS about our remarkable reusable inner-space outer-spacecraft," Sullivan said in a statement.

She had become only the eighth person in the world to reach that depth. It was just one of many honors she has received in her lifetime. Sullivan's other honors have included being appointed to the National Science Board. She has been inducted into the Astronaut Hall of Fame, National Aviation Hall of Fame, Ohio Women's Hall of Fame, and Ohio Veterans Hall of Fame. She has been awarded the Aviation Week & Space Technology Aerospace Legend Award, National Science Board's Public Service Award, Juliette Award for National Women of Distinction, Lone Sailor Award, NASA Medal for Outstanding Leadership, AIAA Haley Space Flight Award, two NASA Exceptional Service Medals, and many other awards.

Guinness World Records recognized her in 2020 with the award for the "greatest vertical extent traveled by an individual [within Earth's exosphere]" considering her work in space and diving to Challenger Deep. She has written and co-written several books, including Generative Leadership: Shaping New Futures for Today's Schools and To the Stars! Today, Sullivan continues to explore the ocean as well as encourage individuals. She also hosts a podcast called Kathy Sullivan Explores.

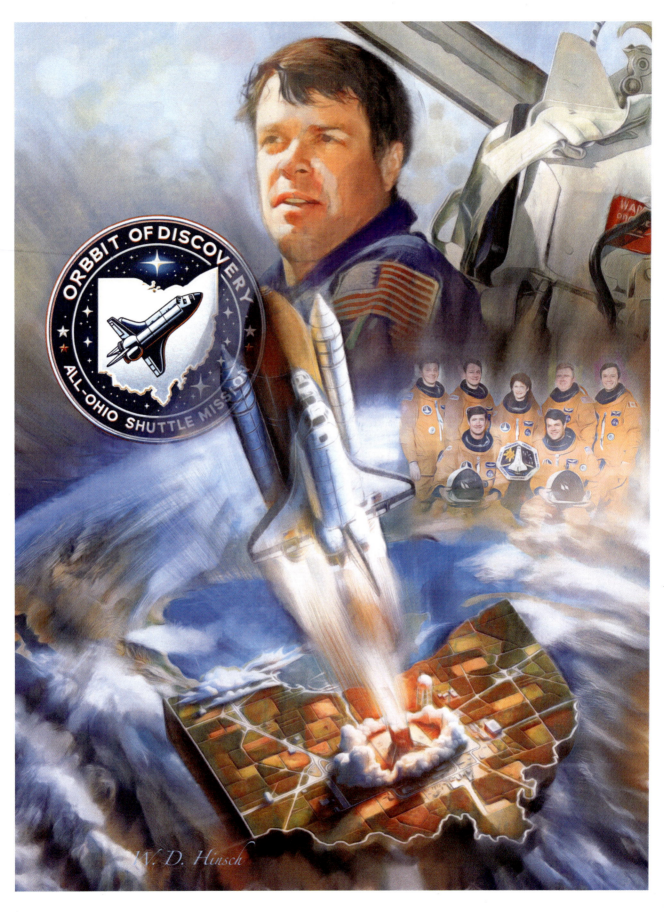

Pioneer of the Skies: A tribute to the courage and dedication of one who has broken barriers and paved the way for future exploration.

Kevin Kregel

"Kevin Kregel's path from New York to honorary Ohioan highlights his adventurous essence. His passion for space led him to the U.S. Air Force Academy and a pilot career, where he flew various aircraft and attended test pilot school. At NASA, he was pivotal in four space shuttle missions, piloting Discovery and commanding Columbia and Endeavour. His playful yet committed demeanor earned him the title of honorary Ohioan during a unique mission. After NASA, Kregel pursued his aviation passion with Southwest Airlines, underscoring his enduring commitment to exploration and flight."

When astronaut Kevin Kregel received the proclamation that he was an honorary Ohioan, he had just one question.

"Do I have to pay taxes in Ohio from now on?" he asked.

Kregel, who was born in New York on Sept. 16, 1956, enjoyed the playfulness of being named an honorary Ohioan, though his hometown of Amityville put up a bit of resistance. In a good-hearted letter, town officials wrote to NASA, "WE lay claim to him!"

His path to becoming an honorary Ohioan began when he was assigned to a flight with four other astronauts, all of whom hailed from the Buckeye State. When the crew found this out, they thought it was a good idea to write to Ohio's governor to see if he would make Kregel an honorary Ohio citizen, making the 1995 shuttle mission a true "all-Ohio crew."

Kregel's journey to the space program began when he was young, watching the Mercury, Gemini, and Apollo programs and enjoying science fiction books. He graduated from the U.S. Air Force Academy in 1978 with a Bachelor of Science degree in astronautical engineering. He then earned his pilot wings in 1979. He was assigned to an F111 aircraft at RAF Lakenheath; as an exchange officer he also flew an A-6E aircraft. Kregel then did an exchange tour at the U.S. Naval Test Pilot

School. He was assigned to conduct weapons and electronic system testing on the F111 and F15 and did the initial weapons certification test for the F15E.

Kregel resigned from active duty in the Air Force in 1990 to work for NASA as an aerospace engineer and instructor pilot. His primary responsibilities in that position were to conduct initial flight tests of the T38 avionics upgrade aircraft and act as an instructor pilot in the shuttle training aircraft. In 1992, he was accepted to the astronaut program. He had several technical duties, including being part of the astronaut support personnel team, and being a deputy for the Astronaut Office Space Station Branch and the Orbital Space Plane Project.

Kregel's first mission to space was onboard Discovery in July 1995. He was the pilot on the flight. It was during training for the mission —t hat was to deploy the Tracking and Data Relay Satellite and do experiments — that the other four members of the crew realized they were all from Ohio.

According to the book, Orbit of Discovery, it was noted that Kregel was a good sport about being an honorary Ohioan, talking about the perks.

"Butter cows, Stadium Mustard, and Chief Yahoo [the then Cleveland American League Baseball mascot]," he listed. Fellow crew member Donald Thomas later quipped that Kregel got "hooked" on Stadium Mustard during the flight.

Mission Control once asked him if the rest of the crew from Ohio was giving him any trouble.

"One New Yorker can easily handle four Ohioans," he joked, laying on an extra thick New York accent.

There was plenty of work to do on the mission. Kregel took part in the biological research canister experiment to study the effects of microgravity on the physiological processes in plants, insects, and small inveterate; the window experiment to work on an understanding of chemistry and dynamics of low-Earth orbit; and a radiation monitoring experiment to measure the exposure to ionizing radiation on the shuttle. Discovery's nine-day mission ended as the shuttle touched down on July 22, 1995.

Kregel went into space three more times during his career at NASA. His next flight was a year later, on board Columbia. The fifteen-day mission dealt with the life and microgravity Spacelab mission. The shuttle lifted off on June 20, 1996, with Kregel as pilot. Spacelab and Earth observations were Kregel's primary responsibilities on the mission. The flight was the first to have a tiny video camera mounted to the shuttle's forward flight deck. The footage focused on Commander Tom Henricks and Kregel from launch until the shuttle reached orbit.

Kregel's third flight was on board the Space Shuttle Columbia in November 1997. The flight, in which Kregel was a commander, included another microgravity payload with experiments.
Among the experiments was one about different plant growth.

"We're looking at the effects that microgravity and radiation have on plants and their pollination because when we go to space for longer lengths of time, we're probably going to have to grow our own plants for food," Kregel said during a post-flight presentation at NASA.

The crew spoke with President Bill Clinton, who wished the crew a happy Thanksgiving.

"Well, sir, we really feel great, and, of course, we miss our own families down on Earth, but the six of us up here are a family in itself, so we're enjoying this Thanksgiving Day also," Kregel said, adding a thank you to all the thousands of men and women who help support the space program and future of the ISS.

One part of the mission did not go as planned. A Spartan-201 sun-study satellite was deployed that was supposed to make a slow turn after it was deployed and then observe the sun. When the crew tried to retrieve the satellite, it went into a spin due to a computer glitch and the satellite didn't capture any data on the sun. A spacewalk had to take place to recover the satellite.

"A big success of that incident was [that] in a short time frame, all the folks getting together, coming up with a plan to retrieve a very valuable asset," Kregel said during a post-flight presentation. "And if that doesn't show the ability of humans to adapt to changing situations in space, then I don't know what is. So in a lot of ways it was a big success."

Kregel said the sixteen-day mission was "very interesting."

"We had a lot of successes," he stated after Columbia's landing on Dec. 5, 1997. "We had a little bit of downtrodden time there. But together as a team ... I think we ended up with a very super mission."

Kregel's final mission was in February 2000, on board the Space Shuttle Endeavour. The eleven-day mission was a shuttle radar topography mission to map approximately 47 million miles of the Earth's surface.

"We're ready to map the world," Kregel said after liftoff. He was the commander of the flight.

Crew members took more than 326 digital tapes containing radar data of Earth's surface. They worked in around-the-clock shifts to keep two radar antennas running. One was in the cargo bay, while the other was held at the end of a 197-foot mast. The antennas collected information on more than 43.5 million square miles that were used to make a 3D topographic map. The crew also did a student experiment called EarthKam, which took digital photos through the overhead flight-deck windows. Pictures were sent to middle school students, who could select the photo targets to be used in various classroom projects. More than 75 middle schools took part in the program.

After his final flight, Kregel was assigned to the Space Launch Initiative project in the Engineering Directorate at Johnson Space Center. He stayed in the position until he retired from NASA in 2003. During his last year working for NASA, Kregel was part of the group of NASA contractors, designers and crew members that examined the debris after the Columbia disaster when the shuttle disintegrated on re-entry on Feb. 1, 2003. Kregel had flown on the shuttle twice in his career.

"You see some of the debris and you see why some pieces survived and others didn't," he told media outlets. "You have all this evidence here that can help [learn about the breakup]."

During his career, Kregel was honored with several awards, including the Defense Meritorious Service Medal, Air Force Meritorious Service Medal, Air Force Commendation Medal, Navy Commendation Medal, four NASA Space Flight medals and a NASA Exceptional Service Medal. After leaving NASA, Kregel has worked for Southwest Airlines as a first officer.

Kregel still enjoys being an honorary Ohioan. He even attended NASA's 50th anniversary celebration in Cleveland in 2008 as an honorary citizen of the state.

The Human Element: Celebrating the spirit of innovation and the tangible impact of space exploration on human progress and technology.

Dr. Michael Barratt

*"Dr. Michael Barratt blends his medical expertise
with a passion for space. After earning his medical degree and
specializing in aerospace medicine, he joined NASA in 1991. There,
Barratt developed Space Station Freedom's medical systems and worked as
a flight surgeon, contributing to Shuttle-Mir and ISS programs. Chosen as an
astronaut in 2000, he first flew to space in 2009 on Expedition 19,
researching health in microgravity. Leading JSC's Human
Research Program, he addresses space travel health risks.
Beyond NASA, Barratt educates and writes about space
and extreme medicine, inspiring many with his
combined knowledge of medicine
and space exploration."*

Sometimes an education in Ohio can take you to the heavens. As a doctor and an astronaut, Dr. Michael Barratt knows this to be true. Barratt specializes in aerospace medicine and has helped develop space medicine programs for the ISS.

Barratt was born in Vancouver, Washington, on April 16, 1969. He wanted to go into medicine because he liked it and enjoyed working with people. He graduated with a Bachelor of Science degree in zoology from University of Washington in 1981 then earned a medical degree from Northwestern University in 1985.

"I started realizing that there was this entity called aerospace medicine, that I loved to fly and do a lot of other things that were sort of outside the normal office routine," Barratt said speaking to the Johnson Space Center's (JSC) Oral History Project. Space medicine was a combination of Barratt's interests.

"I did training in internal medicine mostly to learn pathophysiology in preparation for aerospace medicine, and then entered an aerospace medicine training program at Wright State University in Ohio," Barratt remarked. "This program was run jointly by Wright State University and NASA and Wright-Patterson Air Force Base. It's away from JSC, which in some ways is a good thing, because you learn what the outside world is doing."

Barratt began working at NASA's JSC in May 1991 as an aerospace project physician with Krug Life Sciences, an aero-medical research company that supported NASA's crewed space program. He then worked on medical systems as the manager of the hyperbaric and respiratory subsystems for the Space Station Freedom. Barratt then was assigned as a NASA aviation medical examiner working for Space Shuttle Medical Operations in 1992. A year later, he was one of three Americans who were asked to witness the recovery of the Soyuz spacecraft in Kazakhstan.

"So that was a wonderful experience," Barratt stated. "We had no idea at that point that would roll into the Russians being a very large force in our space station project or myself living in Star City for a year and a half, as it turns out. But it was a very eye-opening experience for me."

In 1994, Barratt was assigned to the Shuttle-Mir program and was sent to work and train at the Cosmonaut Training Center in Star City, Russia. Barratt was a flight surgeon and said that the Russians were very "anxious to share ideas and experiences." He and other flight surgeons learned things that they never knew happened or even could happen.

"We had a different philosophy on selection and certification and medical monitoring, and we often had disagreements about whose standards should be applied to, for instance, a U.S. astronaut training in the Russian program," he explained. Barratt gave the example that the Russian philosophy was to put crew members in situations such as centrifuge training or sleep deprivation and see how they responded physiologically, whereas the philosophy in the United States was looking at health factors.

"We've learned to make our systems work together," Barratt stated. "We haven't changed the Russian system per se, and they haven't changed ours, but we have learned to merge them into a best-fit plan. That was not easy. That was perhaps the most difficult aspect of my working over there."

During his time in Russia, Barrett and fellow flight surgeon David Ward helped develop a Mir Supplemental Medical Kit to help enhance the Russian equipment on Mir. They also developed training for its use. Barrett became a frequent visitor to Russia as he became the medical operations lead for the International Space Station from 1995-98. He and other physicians developed medical procedures, training, and equipment for the space station. He also served as lead crew surgeon for ISS Expedition 1 using telemedicine.

Dr. Michael Barratt

While Barratt had done a lot of support for space station missions, he was not an astronaut. In 1998, he told JSC that going into space would make him a better flight surgeon.

"Practicing medicine from afar is very difficult, and everything I do is because I am fascinated in what medicine is like in zero gravity, in space," he stated. "I see them before they fly, I see them on video. I see them when they come down, but, boy, even a short exposure to what they go through, to really experience what it's like, it would make me; a, very much better at what I do, and, b, of course, it would be very exciting and be very fulfilling."

Barratt would get his wish as NASA selected him as a mission specialist in 2000. His first flight into space was as part of the Expedition 19 crew to the ISS in 2009. He and others on the crew studied bone loss and cardiac atrophy caused by space, monitored immune system changes, and examined nutrition for staying healthy in microgravity.

Barratt launched on March 26, 2009, and celebrated his 50th birthday in space. In addition to the experiments, Barratt completed spacewalks to add hardware and reposition equipment on a docking compartment in preparation for a new docking and research module. As a doctor onboard the space station, Barratt has been called a real-life Dr. Leonard McCoy, the chief medical officer on the TV show Star Trek. Barratt poked a little fun back at the comparison when speaking to NBC News in an interview about the space station's medical area.

"It's not quite Dr. McCoy's sick bay, but it pretty much has what we would need to respond to the most common and most likely things here," he said. "We haven't really had anything major on the station, so I think we're pretty ready."

Barratt returned to Earth on Oct. 11, 2009, after having spent months in space. His next mission to space would be onboard the final mission for the Space Station Discovery in 2011. During the thirteen-day flight, the crew would deliver the permanent multipurpose model and express logistics carrier to the space station. Barratt helped use the station's robotic arm to install both items to the ISS.

After his return to Earth, Barratt was named manager of the Human Research Program at JSC. The program uses research to mitigate health and performance risks that are associated with human space travel. Barratt's expertise has been used to help train others in how humans adapt to space flight. He is the associate editor for space medicine in the journal Aerospace Medicine and Human Performance, he also edited the textbook Principles of Clinical Medicine for Flight. In addition to these projects, he lectures about space and extreme medicine.

Barratt is still a member of NASA's astronaut corps. He is scheduled to serve as a pilot for the SpaceX Crew-8 mission to the International Space Station in 2024. For his hard work and dedication, Barratt has earned several awards, including Hubertus Strughold Award for Contributions to Space Medicine Research, Joseph P. Kerwin Award for Advancements in Space Medicine, W. Randolph Lovelace Award from the Society of NASA Flight Surgeons, The United States' Air Force Flight Surgeon Julian Ward Award, and many others.

Barratt still talks to students and others to share his experiences in space and medicine.
When asked by the blog Lofty Ambitions for his advice to students who had an interest in space, Barratt encouraged them to follow their interests, no matter what they are.

"First of all, you need to find something you really love and love enough to be the best at it," he stated. "The second thing is to get a good look at the space program, where it's going, what its needs are right now and how you can marry those two. You will find a lot of overlap."

Innovators Afloat: The intersection between science and curiosity, where astronauts and experiments come together to expand our knowledge.

Richard Linnehan

*"From Ohio state veterinarian to NASA astronaut:
Richard Linnehan's journey has led through veterinary medicine,
military service, and space exploration. Linnehan firmly believes that it is
mankind's destiny as a species to reach out to the cosmos and walk among
the stars. He envisions a future where humans will not only reach
out to the stars but live among them for lifetimes."*

Richard Linnehan started out studying veterinary medicine at The Ohio State University and ended up on the International Space Station.

Linnehan was born Sept. 19, 1957, in Lowell, Mass. He graduated with a Bachelor of Science degree in animal sciences from the University of New Hampshire in Durham in 1980. Linnehan received his Doctor of Veterinary Medicine from The Ohio State University in 1985.

After graduating from Ohio State, he went into private practice before accepting an internship that took him to the Zoo Animal Medicine and Comparative Pathology at the Baltimore Zoo and John Hopkins University. Upon finishing the internship, Linnehan became a commissioned U.S. Army Veterinary Corps captain. In 1989, he reported for duty at the Naval Ocean Systems Center, where he was the chief clinical veterinarian for the U.S. Navy's Marine Mammal Program.

Linnehan said he was "lucky" to go up into space.

When the space station was being built, NASA and other officials knew there would be several animal experiments that would happen onboard. NASA put out notice that it was looking for a veterinarian astronaut. Linnehan decided to apply.

He was accepted into the astronaut program in 1992 and was the first veterinarian to complete astronaut training. However, he wasn't the first astronaut in space —

that was Marin Fettman, who went in 1993. Linnehan compared his astronaut training to vet school.

"It was like the first or second year of veterinary school in terms of 70- and 80-hour weeks, studying every night," he told Veterinary Practice News. "It was very intense and very busy."

Linnehan's first trip in space was in 1996 on board the life science and microgravity Spacelab mission. He was part of the Space Shuttle Columbia crew, which would be in space for more than sixteen days conducting various experiments.

"The first mission was half life sciences and half microgravity physical sciences," he explained. "We flew a few rodent cages, but they were mostly along for the ride, we just monitored them. Most of the ... life science experiments were performed on us, the payload crew."

Those experiments included muscle biopsies, strength tests, and more. Linnehan did note that the rats and mice on board did seem to adapt to life in space quicker than the humans.

"They just accepted the environment they were in and learned how to glide around their cages, get food, and hold onto the tiny sphere of water and drink those. It was pretty impressive in terms of how fast they adapted," he noted.

Linnehan's next flight was the second Spacelab mission in 1998 on the Space Shuttle Columbia. Once again, there were experiments on life sciences that focused on microgravity. This time there was also a neurolab, which looked at the effects of space on the central and peripheral nervous systems. Linnehan was the payload commander with Spacelab's systems and sciences being his top responsibilities.

Most of the research happened as planned, but there were issues with the mammalian development team as there was an "unexpected high mortality rate of neonatal rats on board."
Out of the 96 baby rats that were launched, 50 died during the flight. The mother rats wouldn't let the babies feed or did not produce enough milk for them to survive. The sick rats were fed a solution of Gatorade and water by hand to get them back to health. Linnehan motored the rats closely as they were nursed back to health.

"We've still got a bit of morbidity, but things are setting down," he reported. "I think we're OK."

While on the mission, Linnehan presented a lecture at the North Carolina State University College of Veterinary Medicine where he was an adjunct professor. Though the Spacelab missions were over, Linnehan still had a lot to offer NASA. In

2002, he would take his third trip on Columbia, this time as part of the fourth Hubble Space Telescope Servicing Mission. The more than ten-day mission saw Linnehan taking part in his first spacewalk. It was to remove the old starboard solar array from the telescope and install a third-generation solar array. He also conducted a spacewalk to replace the power control unit and to install a high-tech cooling device that would allow the use of the near-infrared camera and multi-object spectrometer.

Linnehan also served as one of the two medics onboard the shuttle. The mission returned to Earth on March 12, 2002.

The next year, Linnehan was with NASA when the Columbia disintegrated on re-entry in 2003.

"I lost some friends, but at the same time we must continue to explore," Linnehan said during a nHance Talk podcast. "The space program must go on. The international space program must go on in an international space program. It is the destiny of our species as Steve Hawkins said, as Carl Sagan said. [What] many people have said [including the] Drake Equation is that we need to explore and eventually need to leave this planet. ... It's where we started as a species. It was our cradle and we need to leave our cradle."

Shuttle flights would be grounded for years after the disaster. It wouldn't be until six years after his last flight that Linnehan had another mission. Linnehan's last mission was on the Space Shuttle Endeavour in 2008. The crew delivered the Japanese Experiment Logistics Module and the Canadian-built robot Dextre during its more than fifteen-day mission. Linnehan was the lead spacewalker performing three spacewalks during the mission. The Dextre robot made things a little surreal for Linnehan while he was working. The crew attached arms, a toolbelt, and two cameras as "eyes" for the robot.

"It isn't sci-fi, it's reality, and it's happening up here right now," he stated about the robot.

He also took a bow tie that belonged to Ohio State University president Gordon Gee into space. He presented the tie back to Gee upon his return to Earth.

Linnehan continues to work for NASA with its Astronaut Office Exploration and Integration branches and its institutional review board. He also is on the Johnson Space Center's Institutional Animal Care and Use Committee.

During his career, Linnehan has earned several honors including the NASA Outstanding Leadership Medal, NASA Exceptional Service Medal, NASA Distinguished Service Medal, Navy Group Achievement Award, Navy Commendation Medal, NASA Space Flight medals, OSU College of Veterinary Medicine Alumni Award, and others. He currently is an adjunct professor at North

Carolina State and Texas A&M. Linnehan appreciates his time at NASA, having met a lot of people.

"I've gotten to travel and trained with multinational astronauts and support personnel," he stated. "I participated in four shuttle missions and completed six spacewalks, as well as rendezvousing with the Hubble Space Telescope and the International Space Station. I've had a pretty good career. Another space flight would have been fun, but you need to make room for the next generation."

Linnehan firmly believes that humans will continue to expand their knowledge of space exploration in the universe.

"I do believe that someday people will be born on Mars ...and they will be Martians, they won't be Earthlings. The first Martians that exist in our timeline will be humans," he stated. "That will be the beginning of it [going from the moon to Mars]."

Inspiration Ignited: Illuminating the educational foundations that fuel the thrust of an astronaut's journey into space.

Douglas Wheelock

"Douglas Wheelock: From Army aviator to space innovator, he is a champion Ohio's aerospace contributions. The engineer knows that with a curious mind and heart full of wonder, many great things can be accomplished. He is living proof of that concept as he continues to strive for innovations to lead others to the stars."

Douglas Wheelock may not have been born or raised in Ohio, but he has spent the last few years in the state emphasizing all it has to offer to aerospace.

"Anything that's going to space and going to the moon has to come through Ohio first," stated Wheelock, speaking to Cleveland News 5 in 2019. "We've got 124 companies throughout the state of Ohio that are contributing to the space exploration program."

Wheelock pointed out that the Orion spacecraft participates in test runs at the NASA Plum Brook Research Center in Sandusky. The facility houses the world's largest simulations for space environments, including a thermal vacuum chamber, a spacecraft acoustic test chamber, and a mechanical vibration facility.

"We can fully test out a spacecraft before it goes to space," Wheelock explained. "And it's the only place on Earth we have this chamber."

It's not just the spacecraft that will be making stops in Ohio. At the Ohio Space Forum in 2022, Wheelock said that astronauts may train at the Air Force Research Laboratory, located at Wright-Patterson Air Force Base, near Dayton.

"The innovation here in the state of Ohio has revolutionized how we look at not only the flight of aircraft, but the flight of spacecraft as well," Wheelock said in a NASA podcast.

Wheelock was born in Binghamton, New York, but considers Windsor, New York, to be his hometown. He earned his Bachelor of Science in engineering from the United States Military Academy at West Point in 1983 and his Master of Science in aerospace engineering from Georgia Tech in 1992. Following his graduation from West Point, Wheelock was commissioned as a second lieutenant in the Army Infantry in 1983. The following year, he entered flight school and was designated an Army aviator in 1984.

Wheelock was then sent to the Pacific with the 9th Cavalry, serving in various capacities. After his time in the Pacific, he was assigned as an advanced weapons research and development engineer to the Aviation Directorate of Combat Development. Later, he attended the U.S. Navy Test Pilot School and was assigned to work at the Army Aviation Technical Test Center as an experimental test pilot. He also served as a division chief for testing airborne signal and imagery intelligence systems to help support the National Program Office for Intelligence and Electronic Warfare.

NASA was his next stop as commander of the U.S. Army Space and Missile Defense Command — NASA Detachment. The command supports NASA operations, providing engineering expertise, developing space awareness, and more. In 1998, Wheelock started astronaut candidate training. Prior to his spaceflights, he acted as the Russian liaison for the Astronaut Office Internal Space Station Operations Branch, was the crew support astronaut for the Expedition 2 and 4 crews on the ISS, and was the primary liaison between Star City in Russia and NASA. During his time in Russia, Wheelock worked with officials with the Energia Aerospace Company to help develop dual-language procedures for ISS crews. He also acted as a spacecraft communicator at Mission Control prior to being assigned to a spaceflight.

Wheelock's first time in space was onboard the Space Shuttle Discovery in October 2007. The goal of the mission was to launch the Italian-built U.S. multi-port module for the ISS. During the fifteen-day mission, Wheelock took part in three spacewalks. Only two were scheduled, the third happened because during the deployment of a solar array, several panels became snagged and were damaged. Another spacewalk was needed to repair the array.

The crew was awarded the Neil Armstrong Space Flight Achievement Award for its outstanding achievements during the mission. Wheelock said his time in space really changed his perception of things.

"I used to dream when I was a little boy what it would be like to live on another planet or travel to another planet," he remarked. He said looking down on Earth from space made him "begin to think of Earth as my favorite planet."

"It gave me a new appreciation," he confirmed.

Wheelock's next space mission would be as part of Expedition 24/25. He traveled not by space shuttle, but on a Russian Soyuz spacecraft to the space station.

"Our increment is going to be pretty busy," Wheelock said prior to the flight. "We'll see a fairly long gap for the next shuttle to arrive, and so we have a fair amount of EVAs, or spacewalks, we'll be doing as well."

He began as a flight engineer, then became station commander and Expedition 25 commander. Wheelock was in space from June 15-November 25, 2010. During his time there, he helped with microgravity experiments involving biotechnology, technical development, human research, and more. He also had to tackle an emergency on the ISS, when half of the station's external cooling system shut down. He led three spacewalks to replace the faulty ammonia pump model that caused the issue.

During his time on the ISS, the crew started beaming down images and launched a "guess-this-mystery-location" photo on Twitter as a game.

"The Earth never disappoints," Wheelock told the Associated Press. One of the photos was of the aurora borealis, which he stated would "forever paint" his dreams.

He said spending so much time in space, he missed not only his family, but also things like rain and the sound of birds.

"It made me appreciate the simple things in life like the sound of rain and the smell of the Earth after the rain," he stated, adding those are absent in space.

Though he has retired from the military with the rank of colonel, Wheelock remains steadfast in his mission with NASA.

"The thing that excites me the most is we're always pushing the boundaries at NASA of what we think is possible, " he said, adding that he feels like he is part of something much bigger than himself.

Throughout his career, Wheelock has earned several honors, including the Defense Superior Service Medal, Legion of Merit Medal, Defense Meritorious Service Medal, Meritorious Service Medal with a first oak leaf cluster, the Army Achievement Medal with the first oak leaf cluster, NASA Distinguished Service Medal, National Defense Service Medal, Russian Medal of Merit for Space Exploration, American Red Cross Hero in Space Award, and many others.

Currently, Wheelock not only works with the space program in Ohio, he also speaks with students and others about space and encourages them to follow their dreams.

"The key is to approach life with a curious mind and an open heart full of wonder about the world around you," he stressed. "Then find something you love to do and then work and study so hard in that area that you live your life with passion and then you live your life with so much passion that people can't take their eyes off you. You can reach the very height of your profession."

Astronomical possibilities

The astronauts in this book have all worked for NASA, but as space exploration grows so does the opportunity to be part of it. While NASA continues to work with international partners, commercial operations also are starting to realize the benefits of space exploration. Ohioans are part of that aspect of aerospace as well.

In 2022, Dayton businessman and technology entrepreneur Larry Connor went to the International Space Station. He had partnered with the Cleveland Clinic and Mayo Clinic to conduct experiments on the heart, spine, brain, and aging in space. He was part of the Axiom Mission 1 crew, which was the first all-private flight to the ISS. In an interview from onboard the ISS to a Dayton news channel, Connor stressed he was not a space tourist.

"Space tourists go up for 5-10 minutes," he stated. "We are literally working 14 hours a day, the rest of time [during the day] is getting a meal and getting some sleep."

As the astronauts have said throughout this book, space travel is the future and Ohio is definitely going to be a big part of that future. Whether through NASA or commercial operations, there will be a need for individuals in many capacities to continue to explore the depths of space. Government officials already have stated there is a need to return to the Moon and then go onward to Mars. As Wheelock stated, "The road to the moon will go through Ohio."

Officials at Glenn Research Center currently are working to develop and test new technology and spacecraft for long-term human exploration missions. People will be needed not only to man these vessels, but to do research and create and test technologies to make safe pathways that will enable humankind to venture farther into the final frontier ahead of us, and know that our opportunities are not limited to what is here on Earth.

Ohioans now and today have a great legacy of aerospace and flight to learn from. While many people across the nation dream of seeing the heavens, Ohioans seem to have a special insight.

To borrow a quote from astronaut Sally Ride, "The stars don't look bigger, but they do look brighter."

For the Buckeye State that seems exceptionally true. Those Ohioans who dream of someday being in space should follow the words of encouragement and advice given throughout this book by the state's space explorers. So, for all those who have a wanderlust to visit the stars, remember these words by Ohioan Neil Armstrong: "Shoot for the stars, but if you happen to miss, shoot for the moon instead."

Acknowledgements

As a young child I attended Space Camp hoping to become someone who walked among the stars. As a teenager, I had the good grace to actually meet and speak with Senator John Glenn. The memory of how humble a man this great legend was continues to shine in my thoughts. While I may have never been an astronaut, my life has had many adventures due to opportunities I seized, even though I was a little scared about them.

With that in mind, I would like to thank Bill Hinsch for the opportunity to work with him and write this book. I would like to thank my editor, Taryn, for her hard work and dedication.

Lastly, I would like to thank my family for their extraordinary support. Thank you all.

Lisa Nicely
November 2023

In commemorating Ohio's remarkable astronauts, this book reflects a joint effort of storytelling by Lisa Nicely and visual interpretation by myself. This rewarding task has been supported by numerous individuals deserving heartfelt thanks.

Foremost, I extend gratitude to my dear friend and exceptional 3D artist, Ed Gabel (BroBel.com). In a previous chapter of life, we collaborated closely, and Ed's expertise in New York City continues to impress. His meticulous modeling of space hardware, like Glenn's Friendship 7 and Armstrong's Apollo 11, enriched my artwork immensely, providing invaluable reference for the Ohio Statehouse rotunda painting.

Equally vital was the innovative scaffold, designed by Ed Delagrange, a lifelong friend and master carpenter. This ingenious structure, with its modular platforms and "barn doors" system, enabled me to safely navigate the expansive 12ft. by 9ft. canvas, a task formidable even when compared to the works of Christy, Wyeth, and Benton.

I owe much to Eric Hennan of Image 360 studio in Perrysburg, Ohio. Not only did he provide the space for this seven-month project, but his contributions in canvas preparation, frame construction, and logistical support were indispensable. His participation in our documentary, alongside his dog Zeke, added a unique flavor, blending humor and dedication.

My family played an integral role. Alex, my eldest, alongside Spencer LeGros and Cory Channel, masterfully created the documentary "The Artist that Captured the Ohio Astronauts," a testament to their creative brilliance.
Emily, my daughter, was instrumental in every stage, from canvas preparation to correcting mistakes to final varnishing, showcasing her artistic prowess. My middle son, Nick, elevated our documentary with his song "Boy from Ohio," capturing the essence of our state and its heroes.

Lisa Nicely, the author of this book, joined this journey when she interviewed me about the painting. Discovering our shared Hicksville roots was serendipitous, and her swift commitment to this book project has been nothing short of extraordinary.

Dan Romano, a trusted colleague of 30 years, was the catalyst. His call in October 2023, informing me about the State of Ohio's request for a painting of Ohio astronauts, set everything in motion. His belief in my abilities led to a creation that intertwines my artistry with Ohio's aerospace legacy.

Finally, the unwavering support of my wife, Carol, has been the foundation of this endeavor. Her resilience, dedication, and sacrifices over forty years have made all of this possible. This book's dedication to her is a small token of my immense gratitude.

This project was a collaboration not just of hands, but of hearts. To all who contributed, your roles have been essential in crafting a legacy that celebrates Ohio's contributions to space exploration. I am forever grateful.

Bill Hinsch
November 2023

About the Author

Lisa Lucas Nicely is an award-winning journalist who has reported on a wide range of topics in Ohio for decades. Recognized as the best reporter in Ohio by the Ohio Society of Professional Journalists, she has also been honored with several Associated Press and Society of Professional Journalism Awards, including those for social issues, investigative, and political reporting. A graduate of Kent State University's School of Journalism and Mass Communications, Lucas Nicely's fascination with space began in her youth. She enjoyed science fiction books, TV shows like Star Trek, and movies such as Star Wars. Her interest led her to attend Space Camp in Huntsville, Ala., where she trained as a mission specialist in orbit simulations. In 1992, during the Ohio 4-H Congress, she had the unique opportunity to meet Senator John Glenn and ask him one, single question: "What's it like for you to look yourself up in the encyclopedia?" Surprisingly, he admitted he had never done so, leaving her amused and him at a loss for words.

Currently, Lisa Nicely works as a freelance writer for several different entities and publications. She resides in Defiance, Ohio.

About Bill Hinsch

Born in Hicksville, Ohio, in 1955, Bill Hinsch has been a professional artist, illustrator, and painter for over five decades. His artistic career took a significant turn in the 1980s when he served as the art director for the Toledo Blade newspaper. In 1992, Bill co-founded Root Learning with Randy Root, contributing as a partner until 2006. He then embarked on a new venture, founding Learning Visuals in 2007, creating Learning Maps and eLearning programs for major companies globally.

Bill's most distinguished work includes a major commission for the Columbus Ohio Statehouse, a 12 ft x 9 ft oil painting featuring the 'Mount Rushmore' of USA astronauts, John Glenn, Neil Armstrong, Jim Lovell, Judy Resnick, and mission controller Gene Kranz. Additionally, he collaborated with legendary aviation artist Harley Copic on an 8 ft painting of Ohio Aviators, showcased in the Wright Patterson National Air Force Museum in Dayton, Ohio, for the centennial celebration of flight in 2003. This event was notable for the attendance of John Glenn and Neil Armstrong, with Glenn signing limited edition prints of the painting, of which Bill is proud to have two personalized copies signed by the great astronaut who was the first American to orbit the earth.

Living in Perrysburg, Ohio, for two decades with his wife Carol and their three children, Alex, Nick, and Emily, Bill continues his artistic endeavors from his local studio, where the Ohio Astronauts were brought to life. His work stands as a tribute to his enduring passion for art and Ohio's significant contributions to aviation and space exploration.

OHIO: The Cradle of Astronauts

Notes